FINISH THE DRAWING

Volume 2

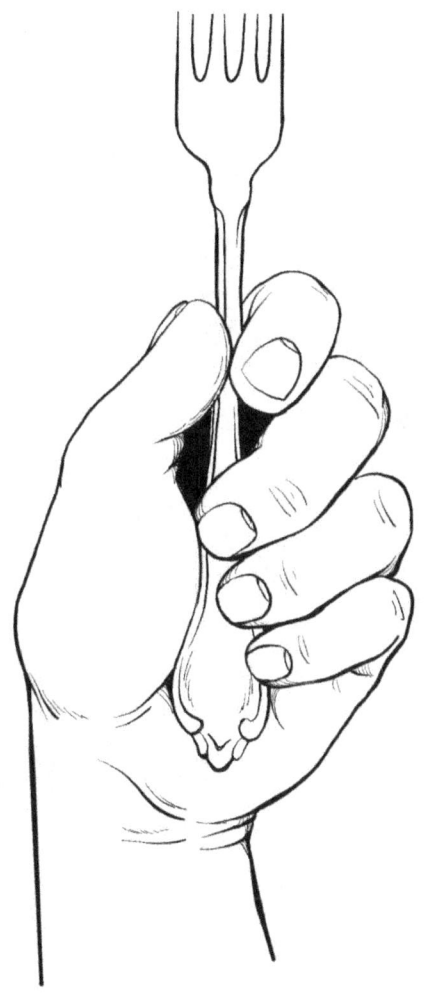

BY

JESS ERSKINE

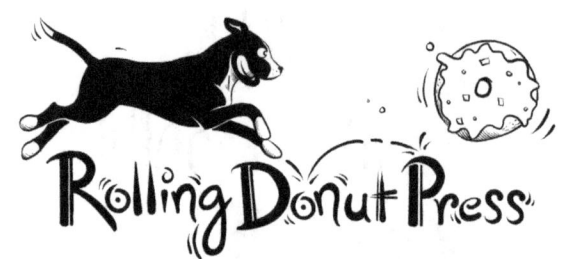

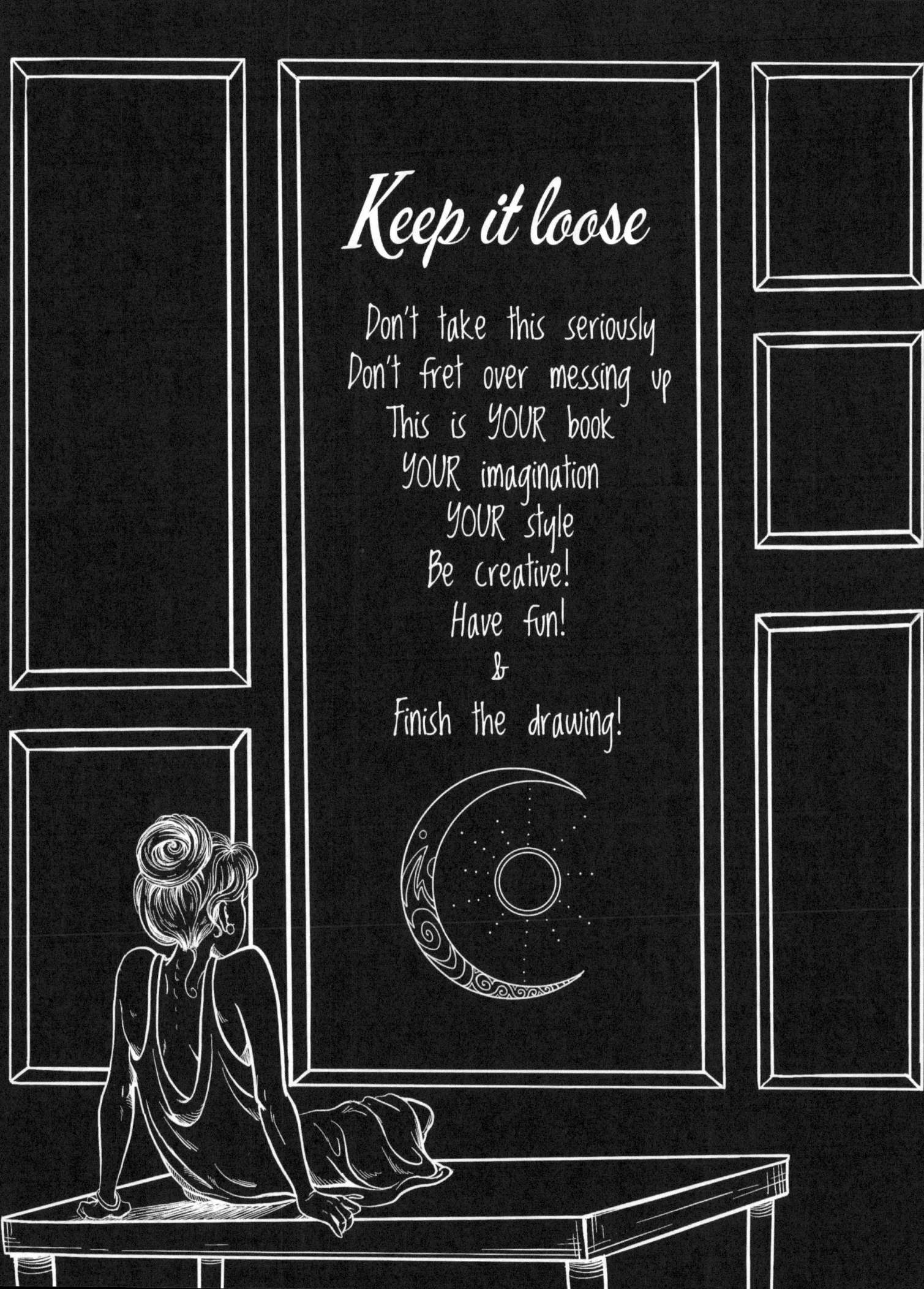

Keep it loose

Don't take this seriously
Don't fret over messing up
This is YOUR book
YOUR imagination
YOUR style
Be creative!
Have fun!
&
Finish the drawing!

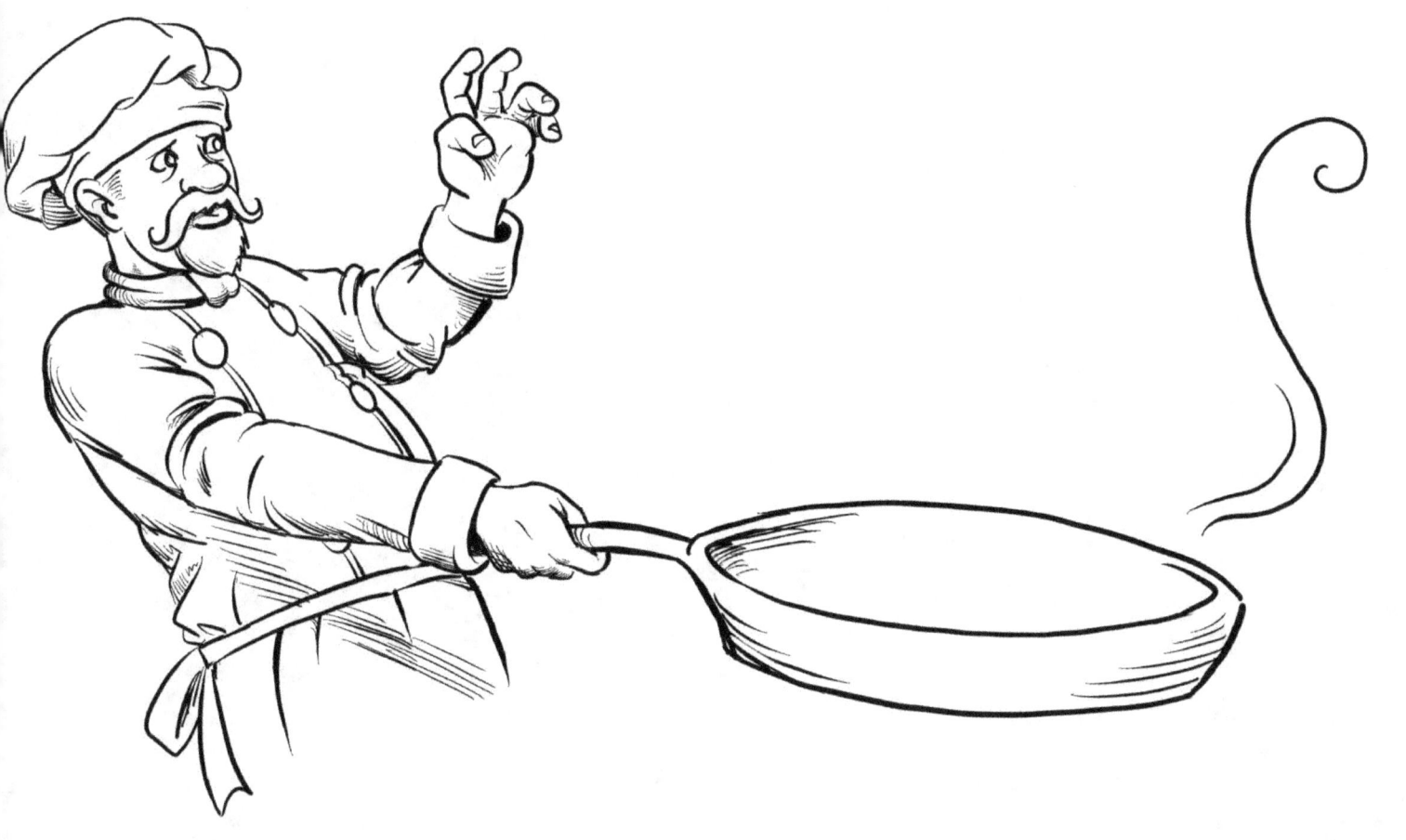

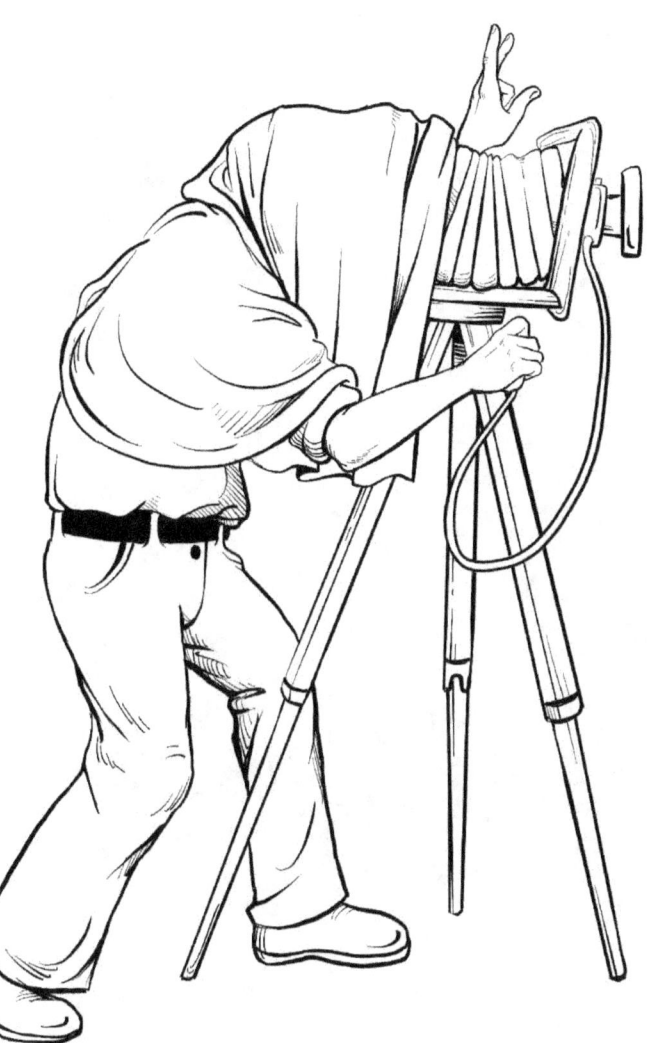

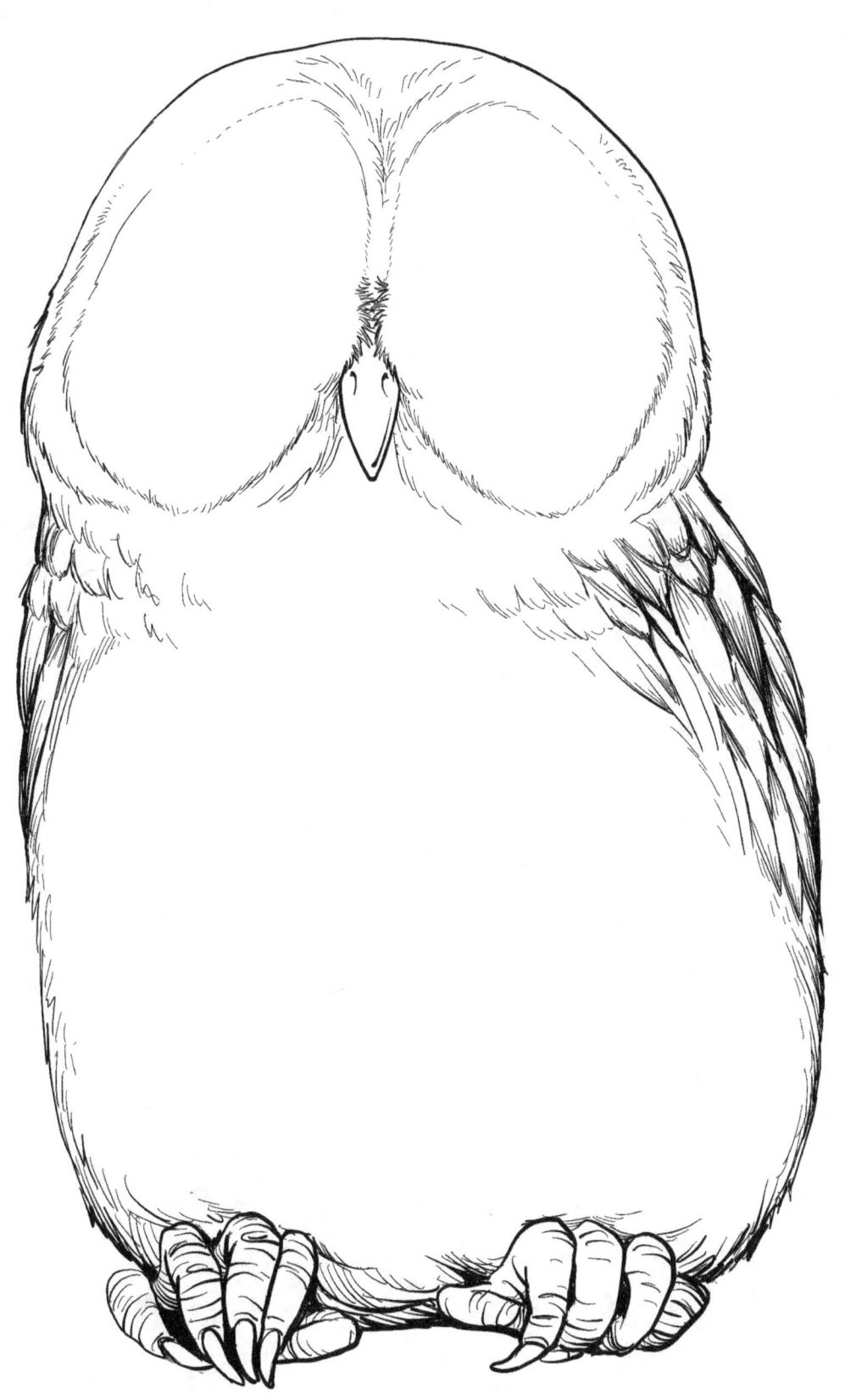

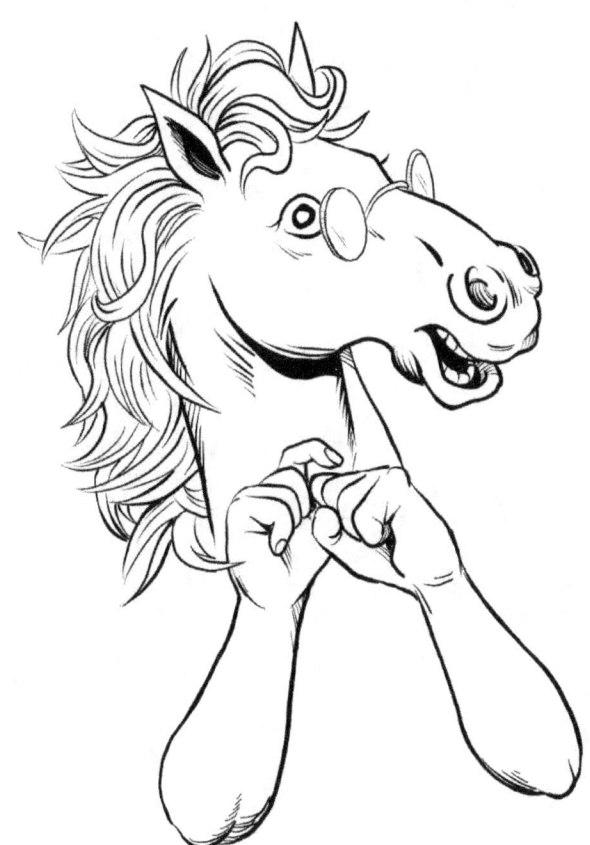

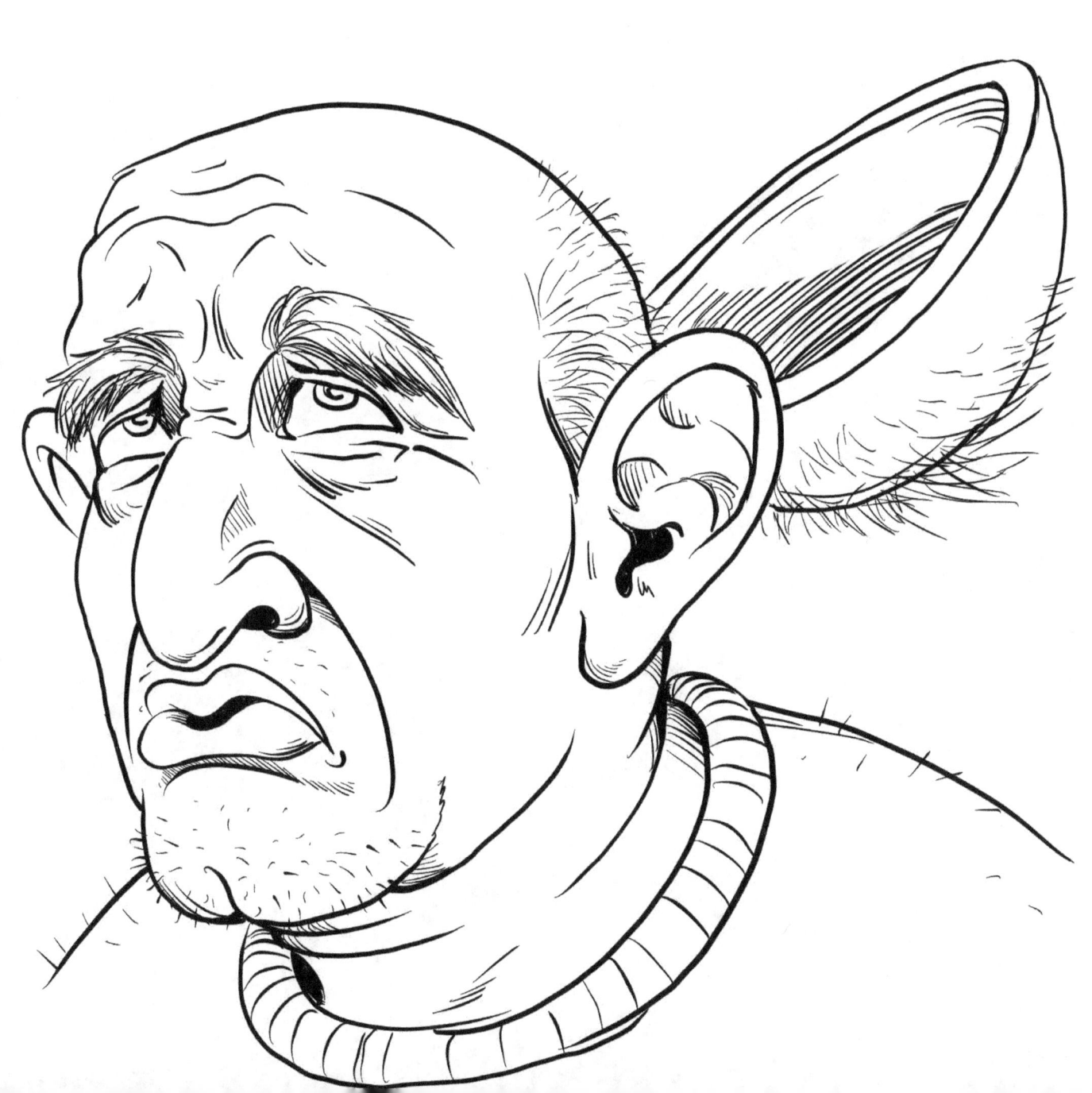

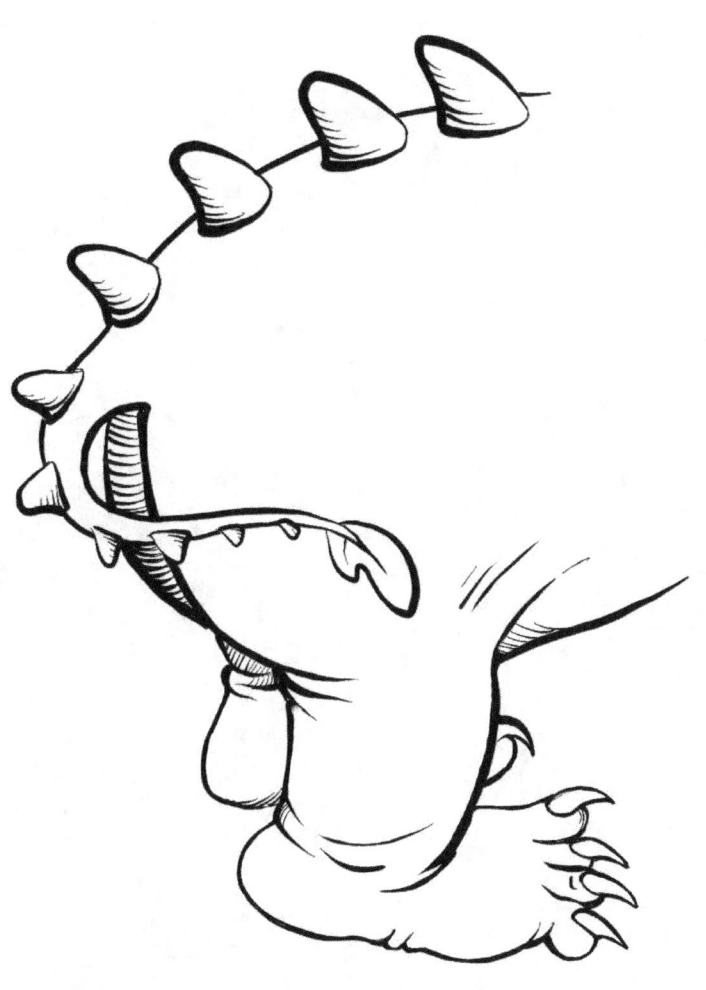

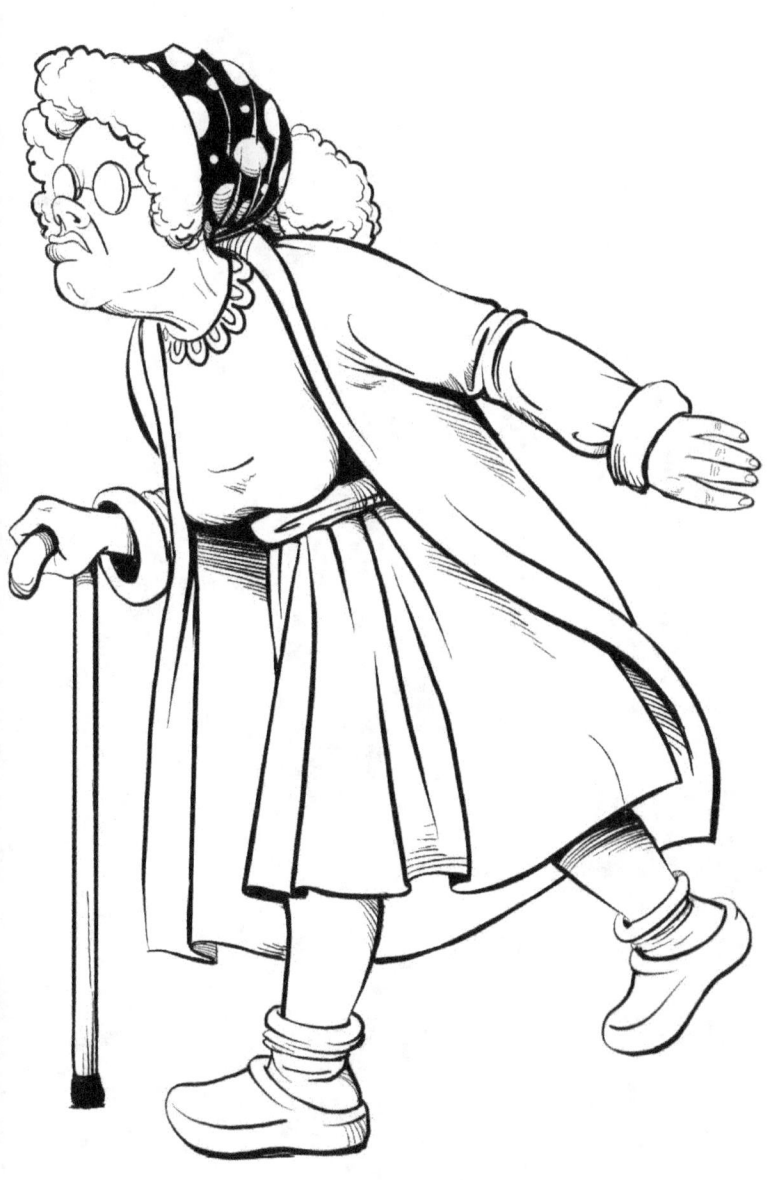

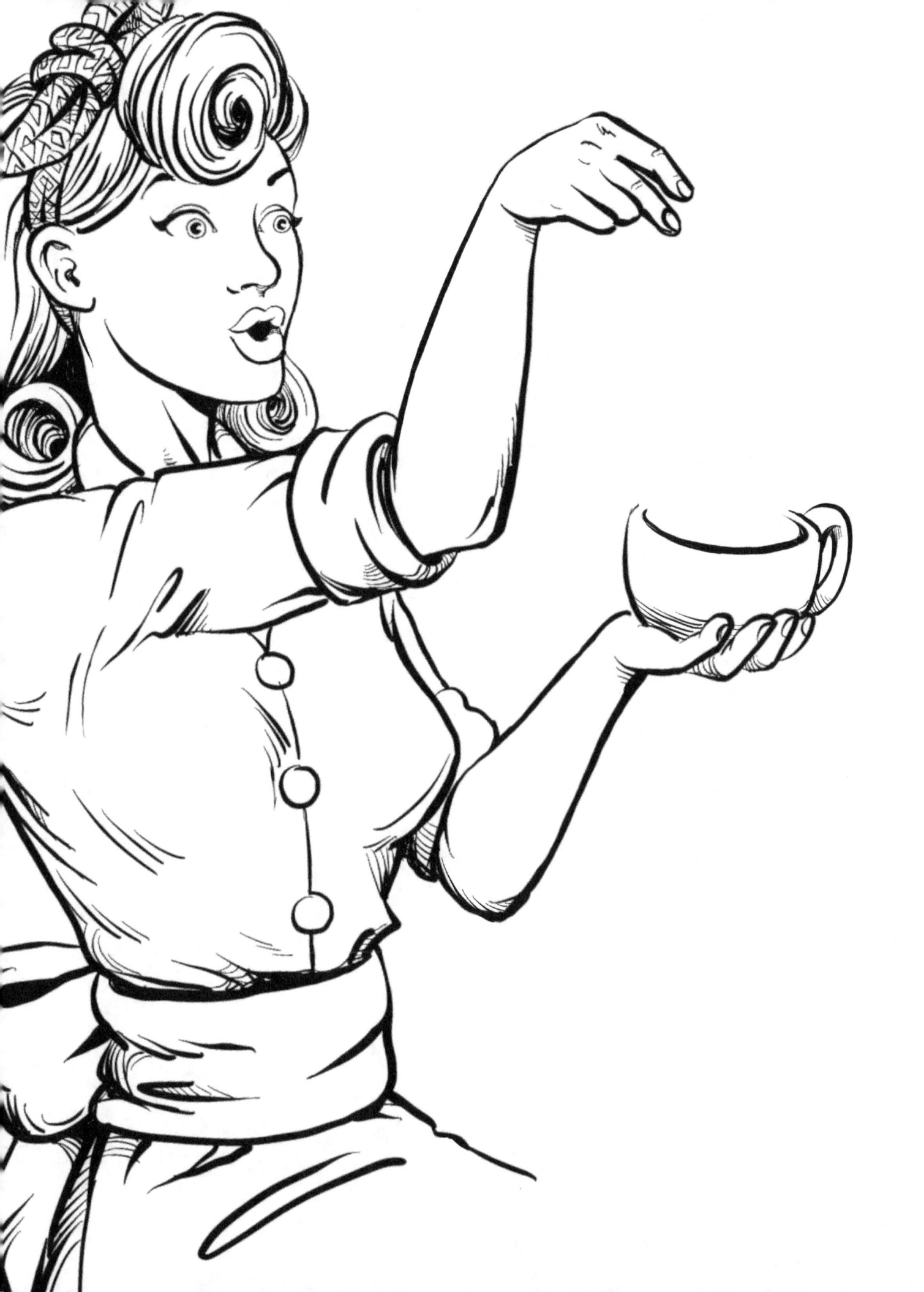

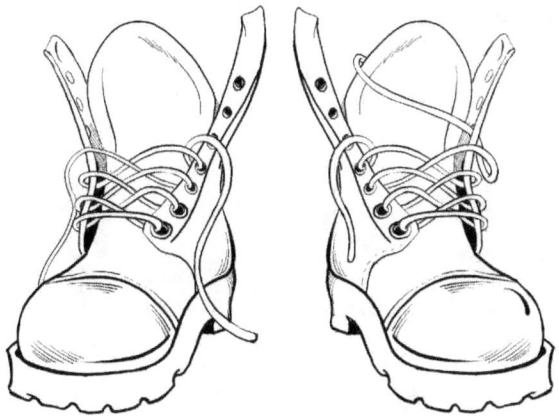

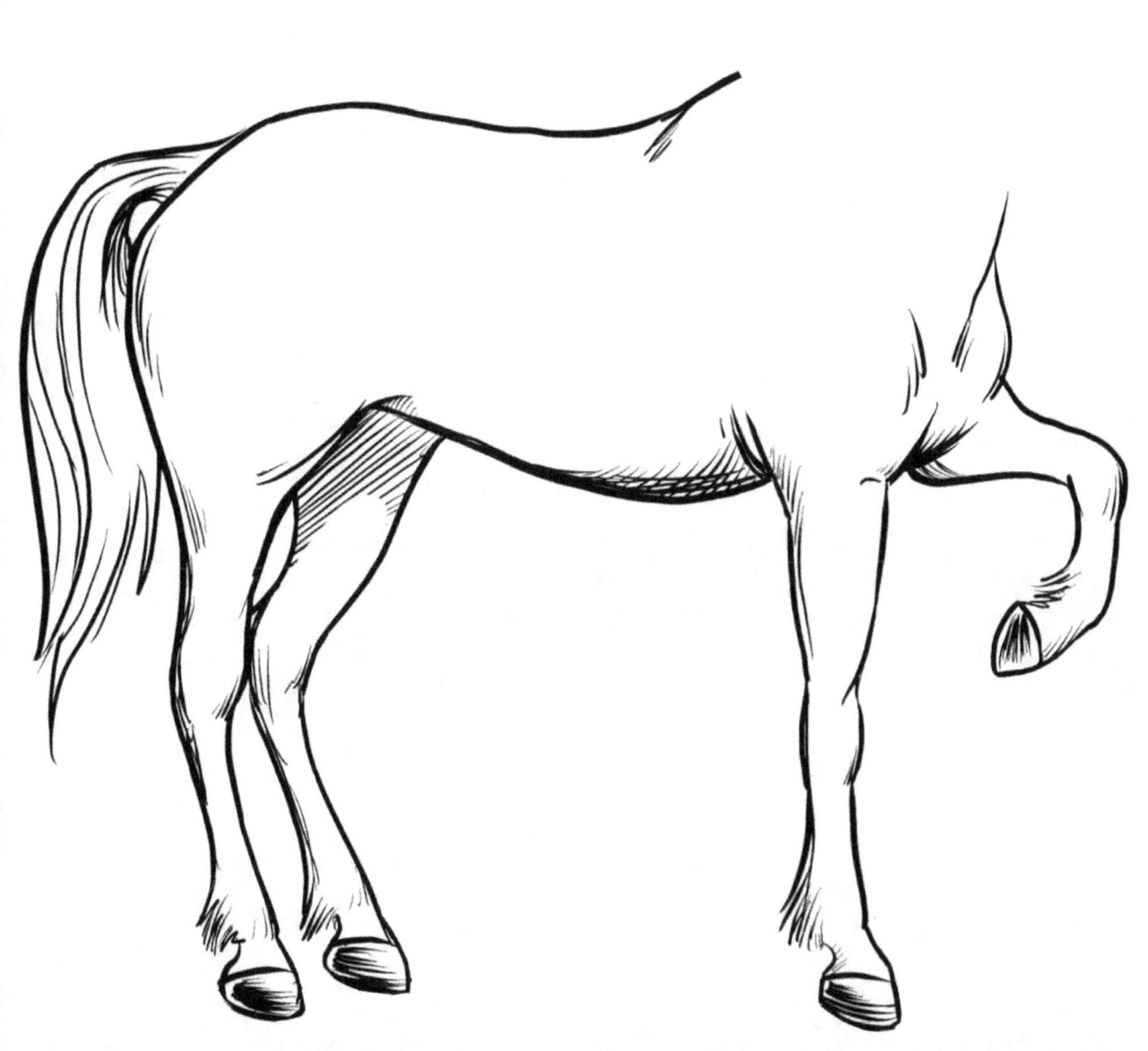

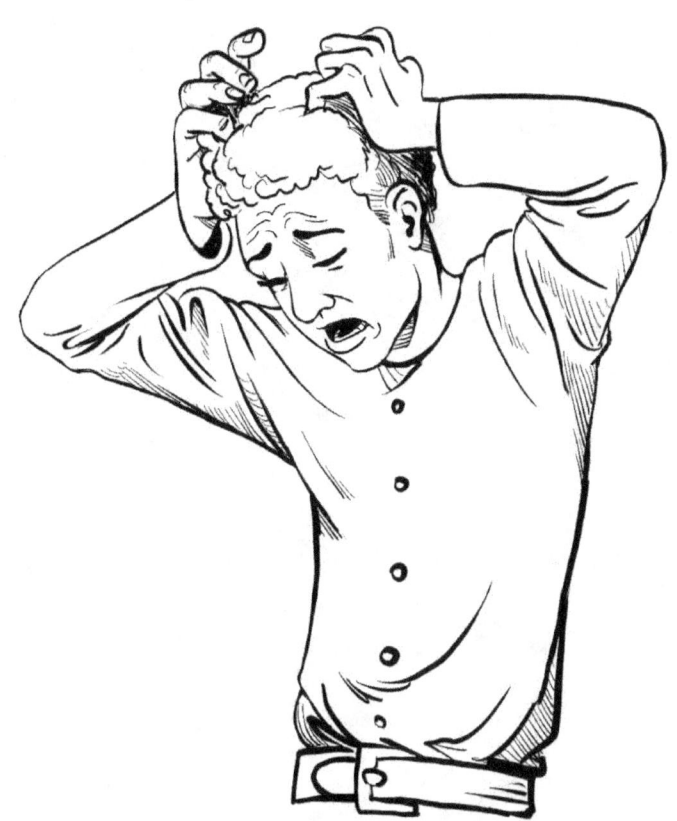

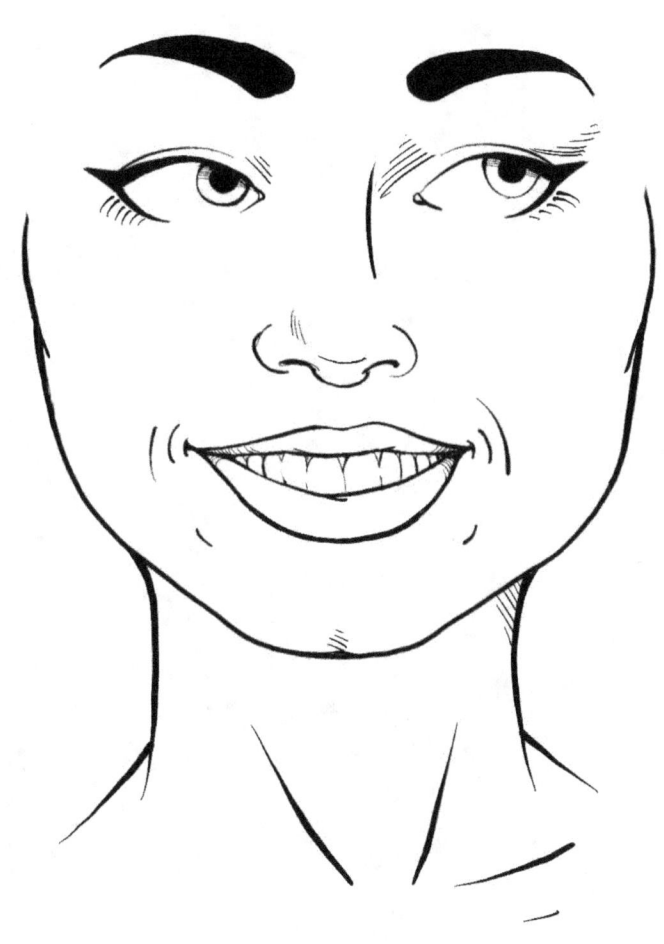

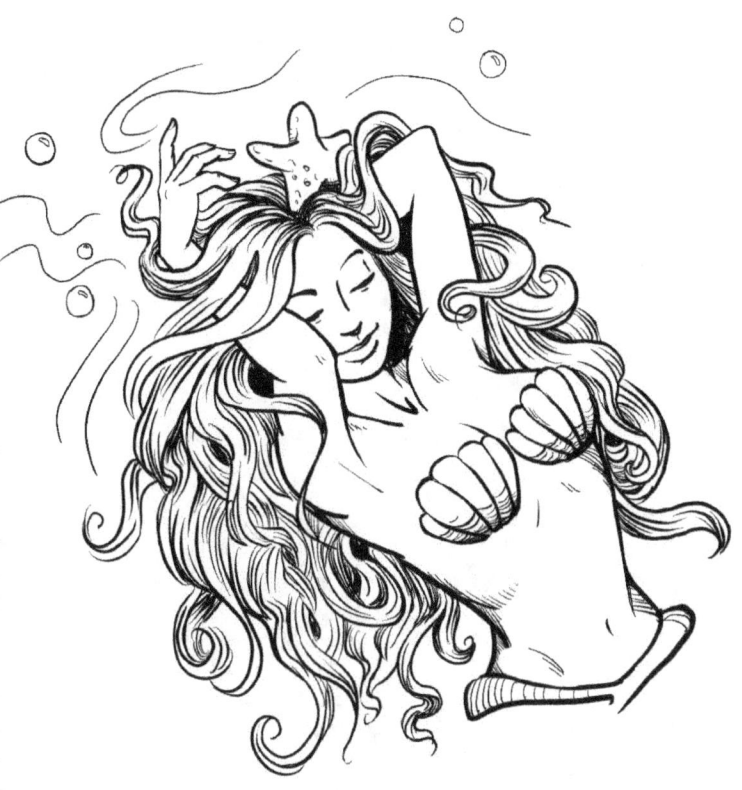

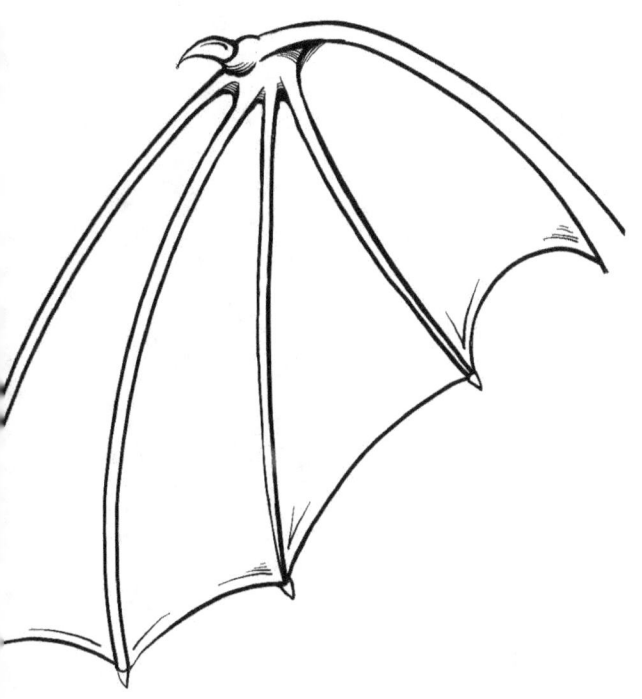
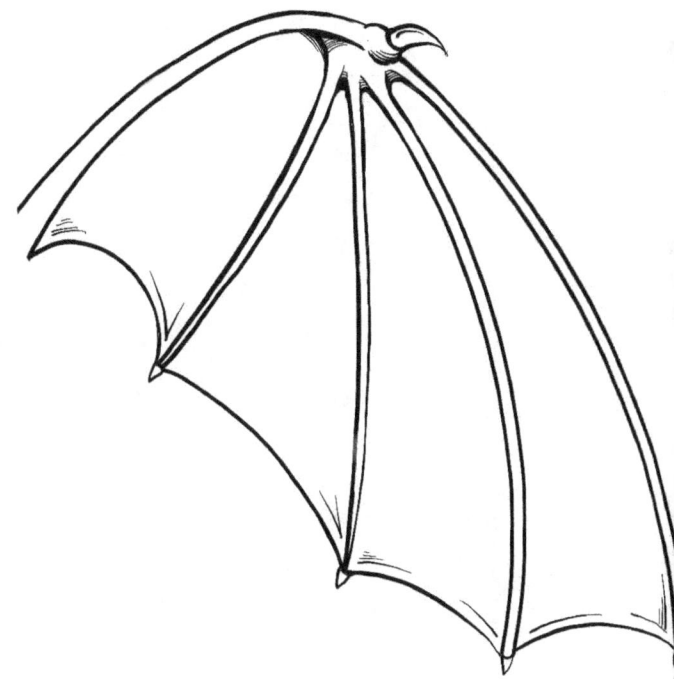

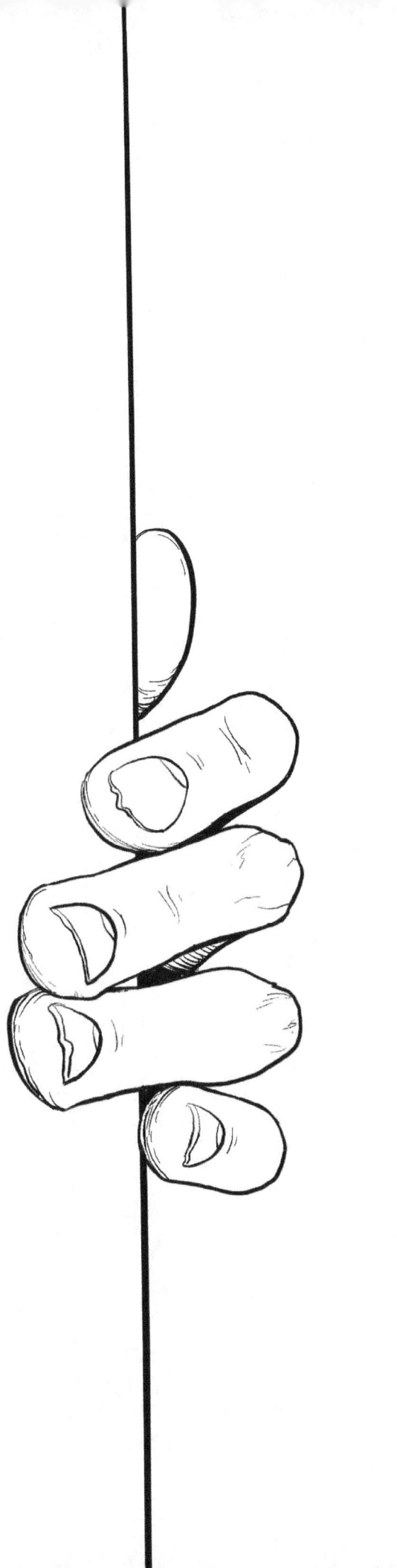

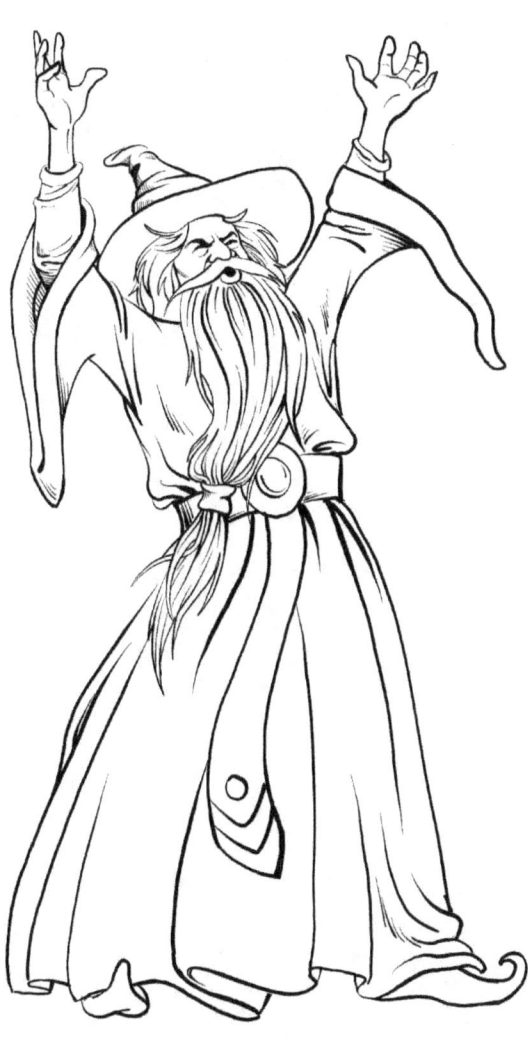

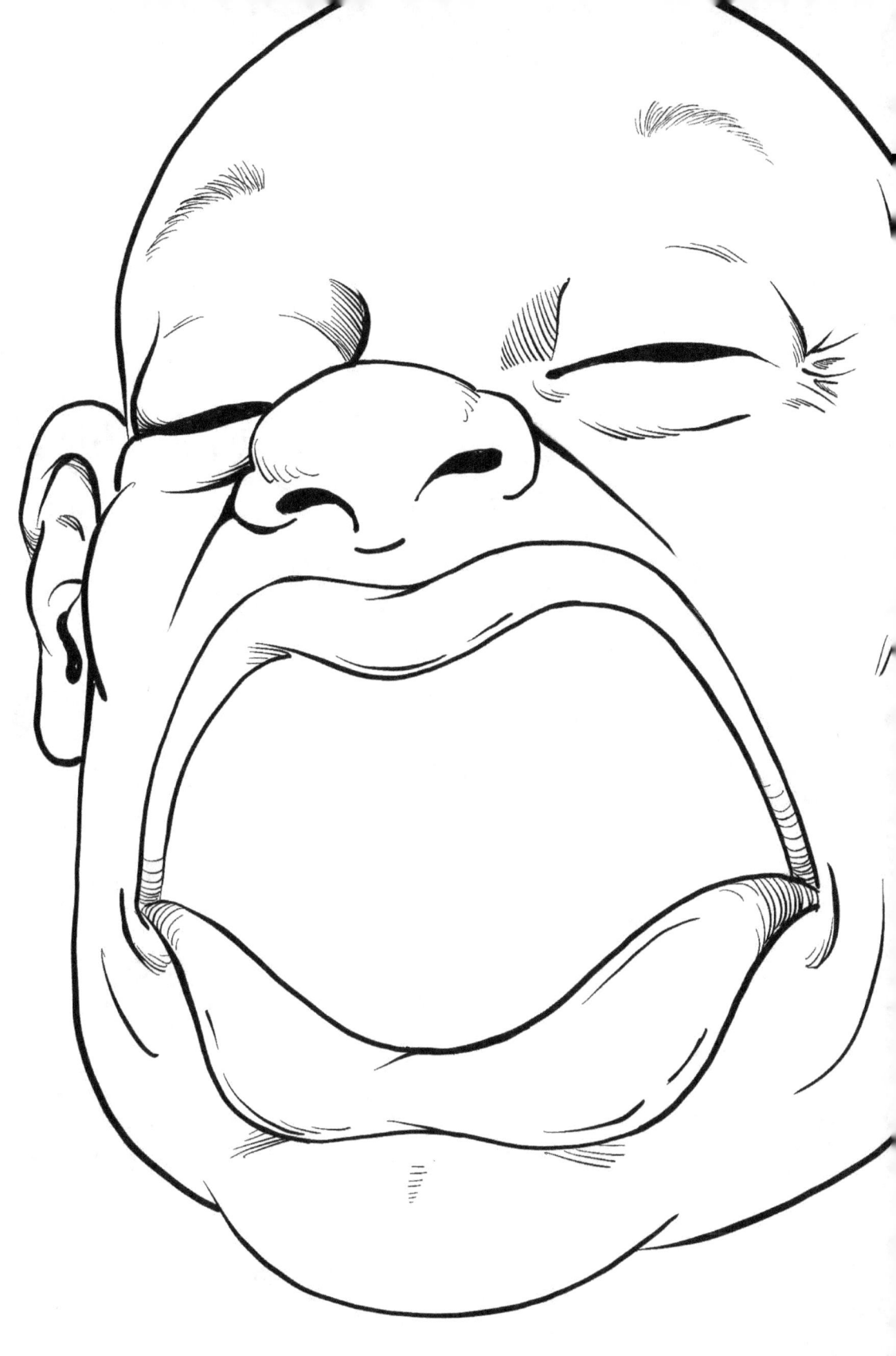

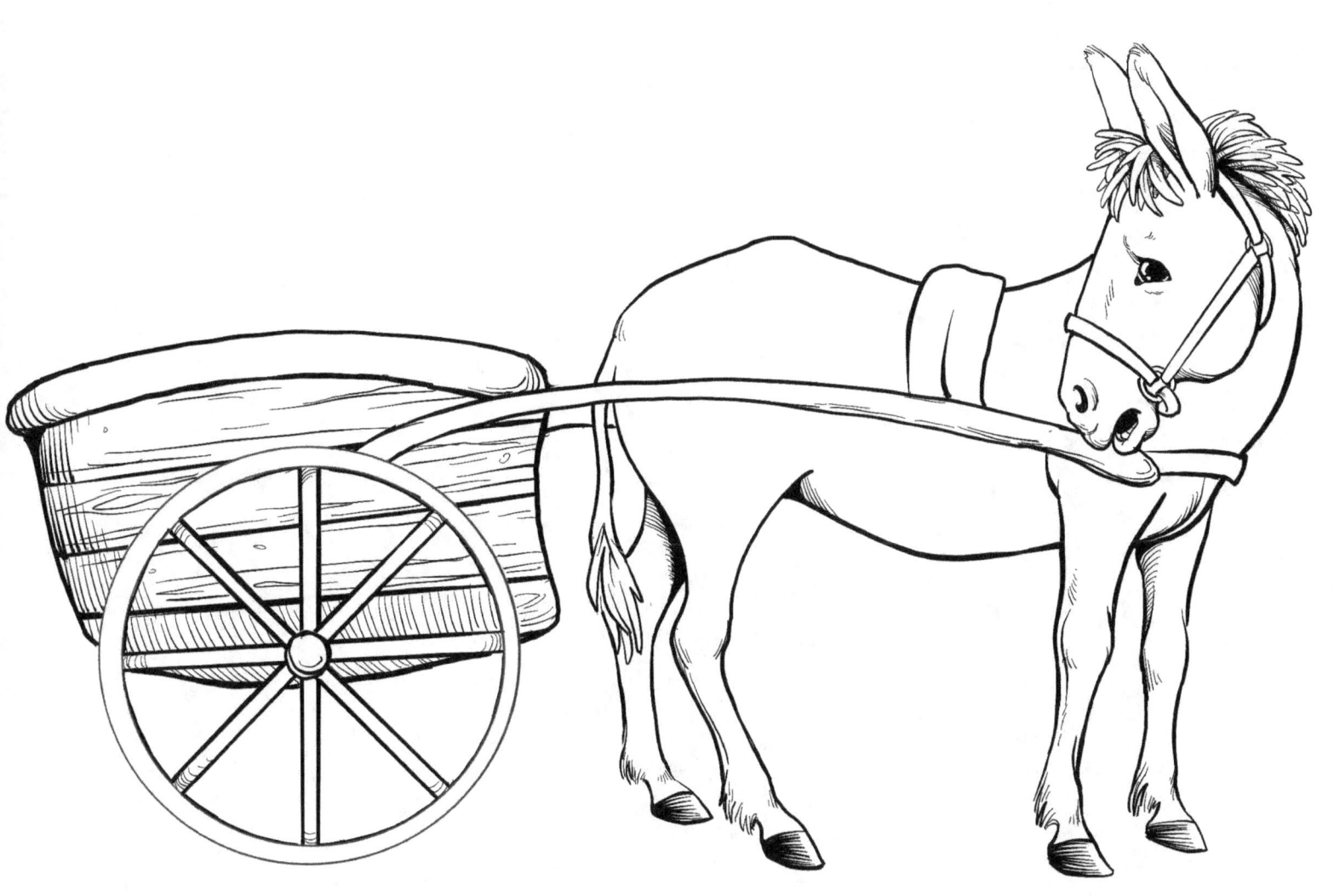

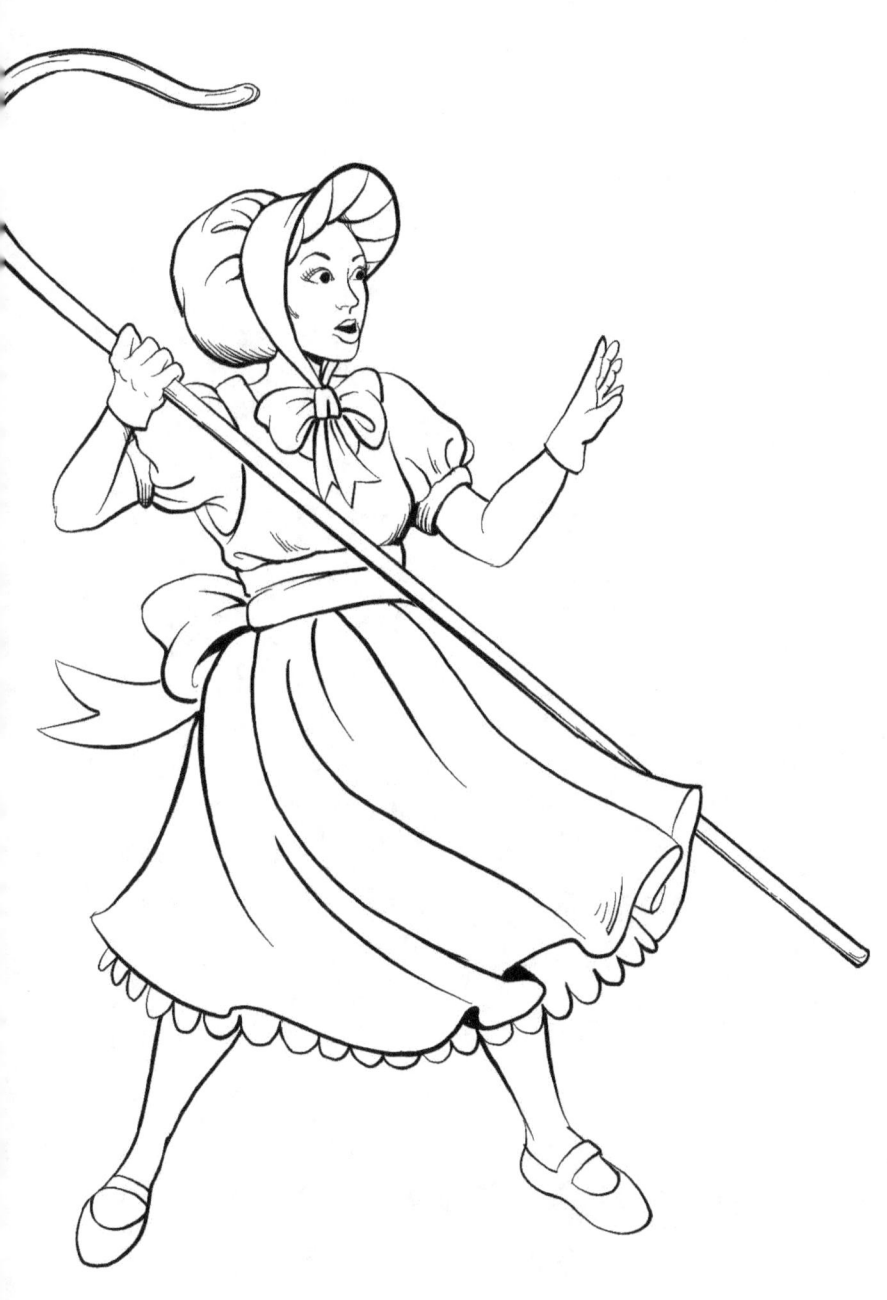

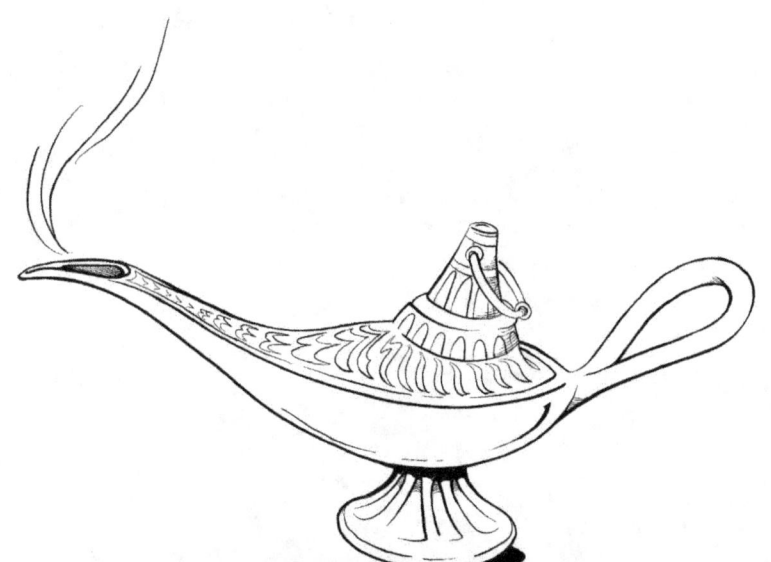

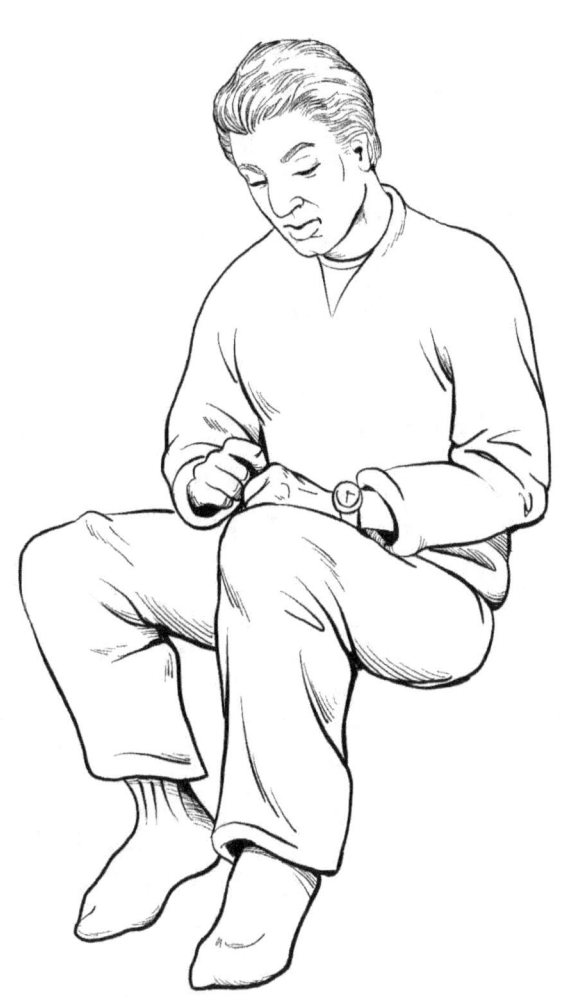

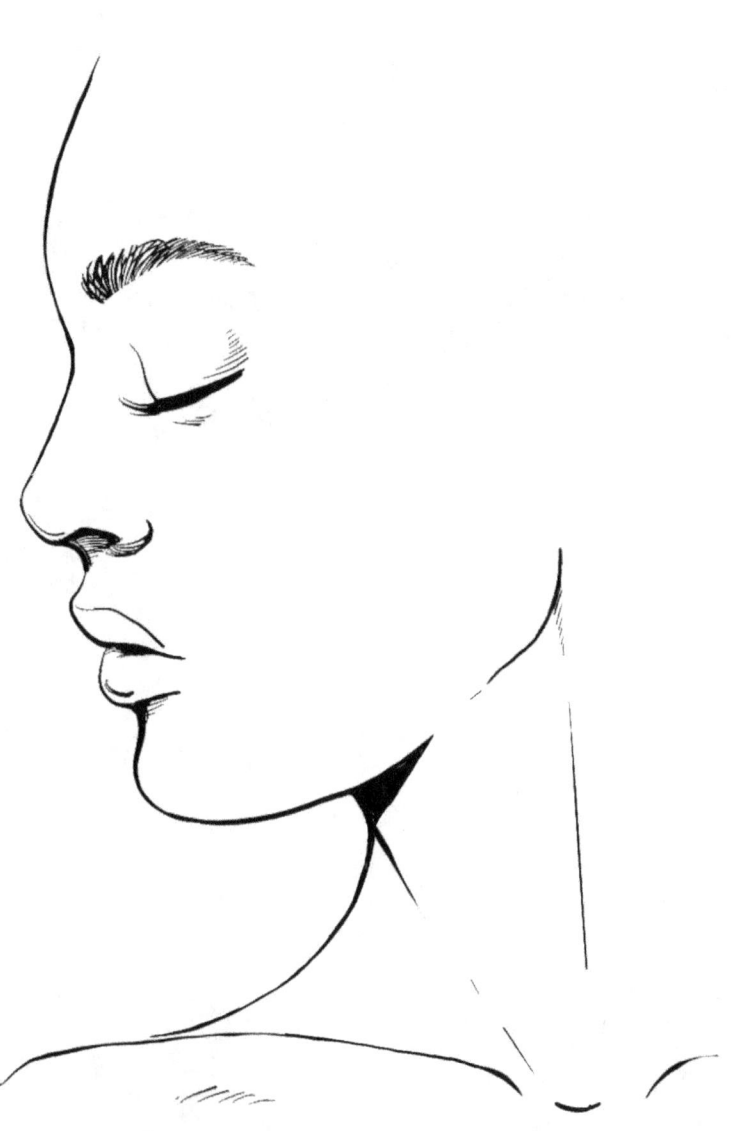

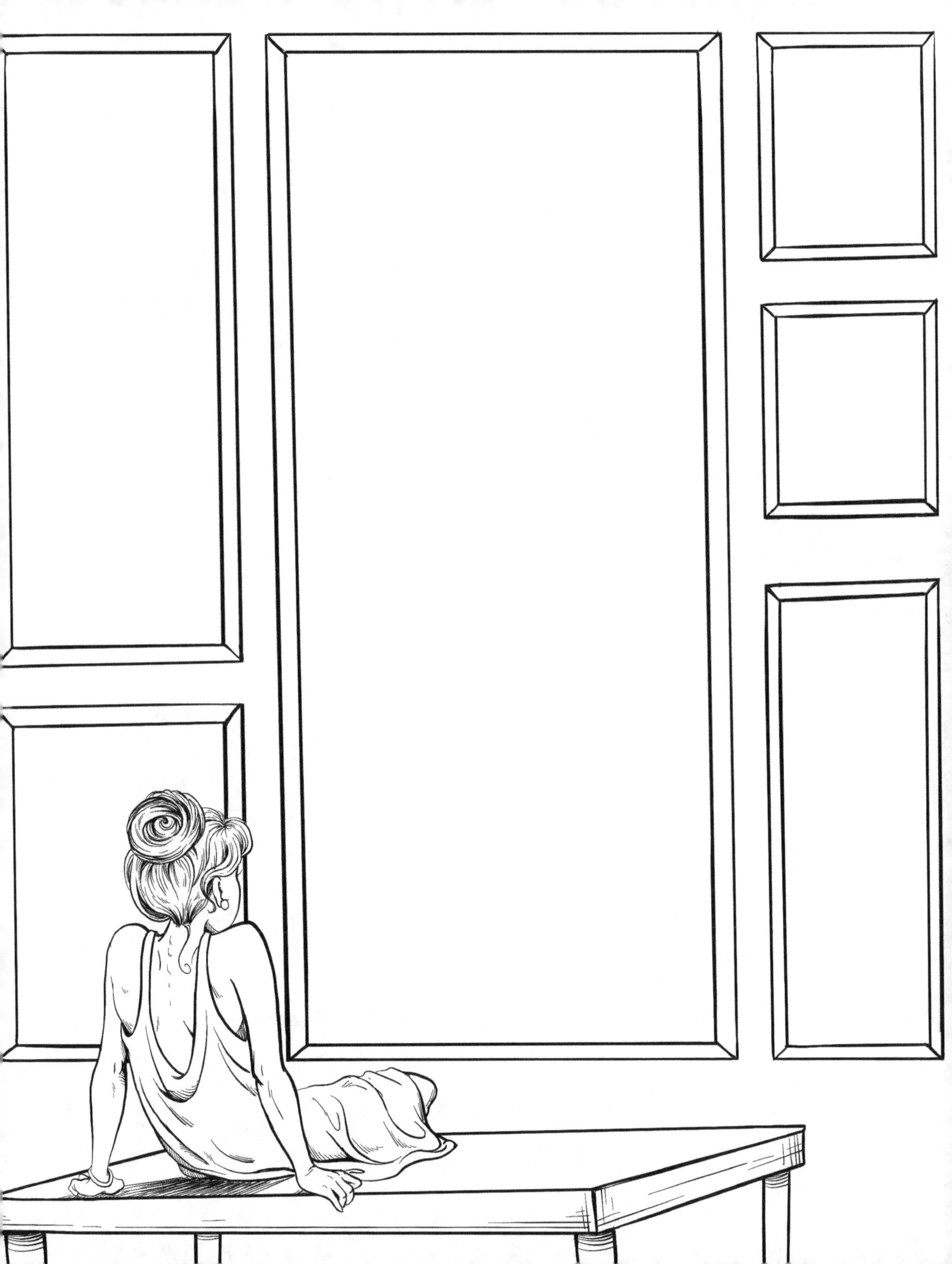

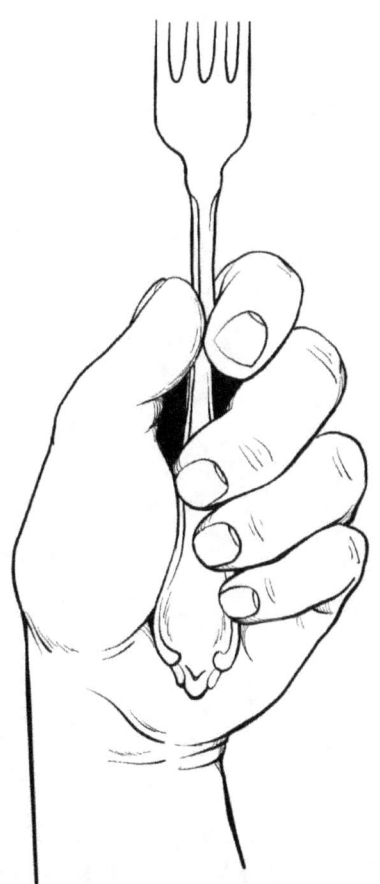

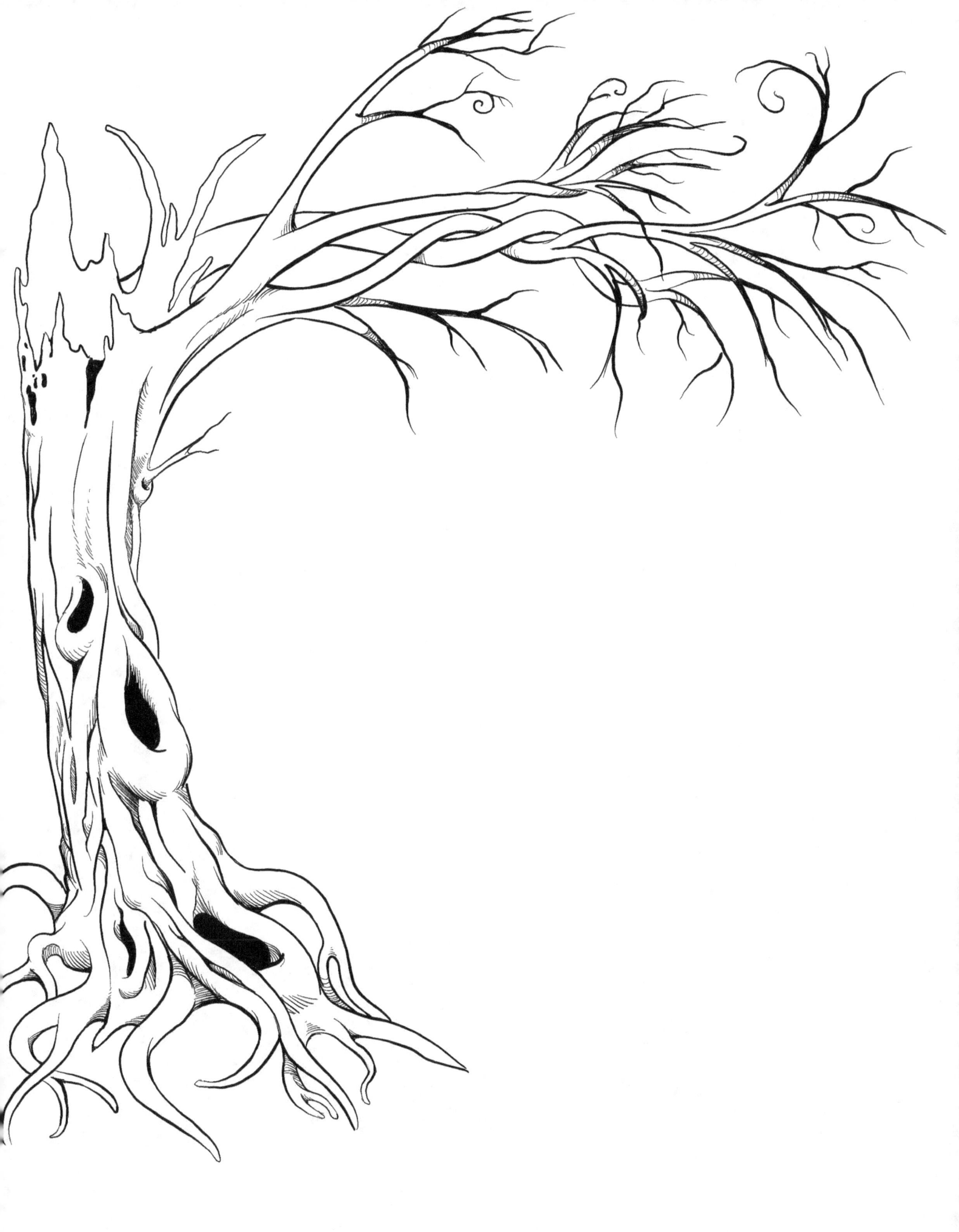

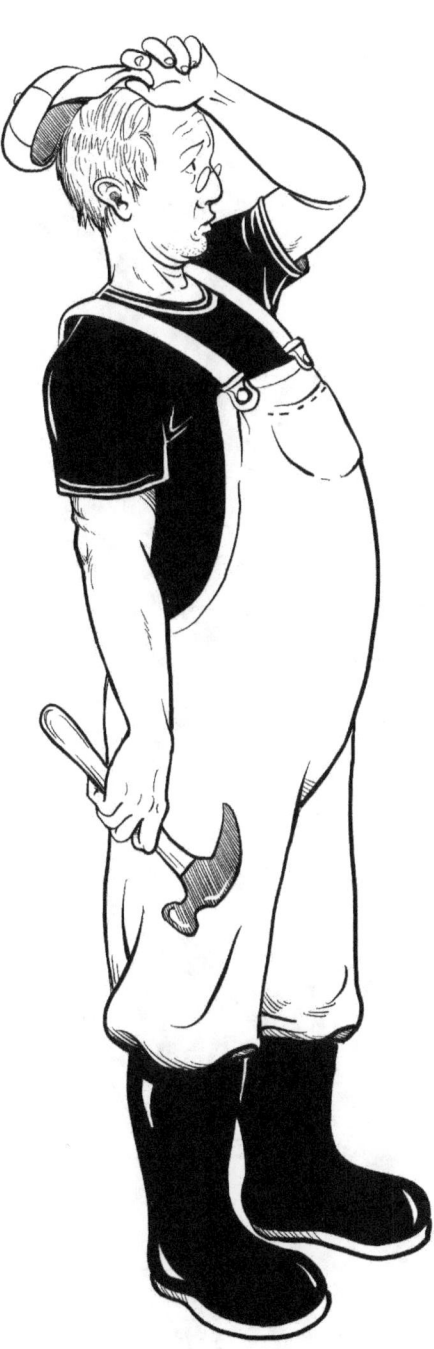

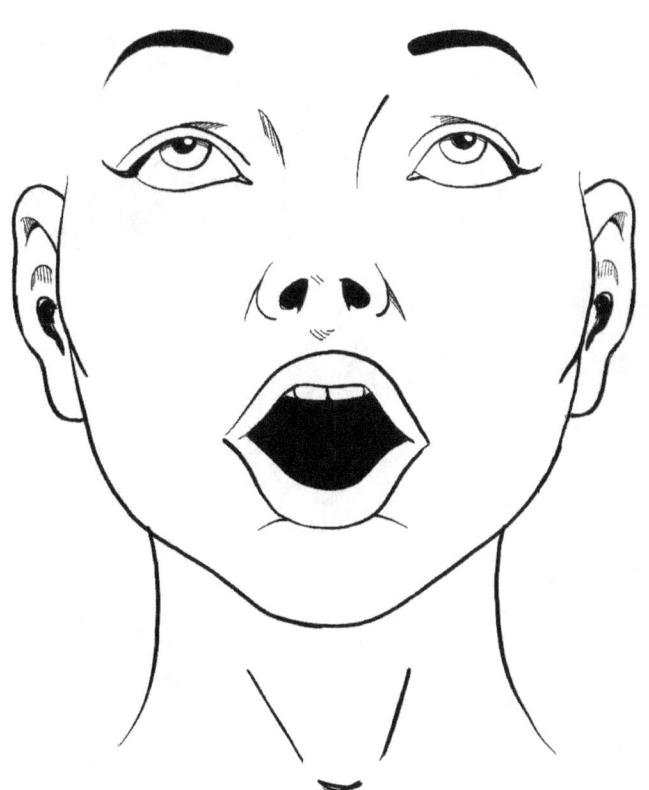

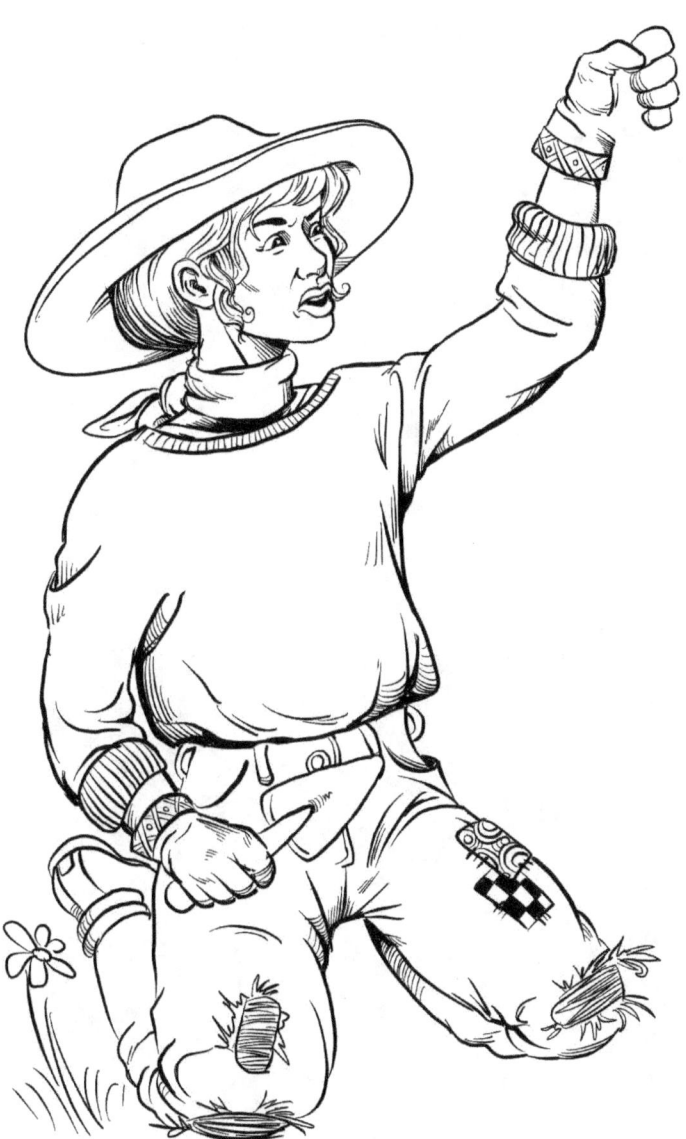

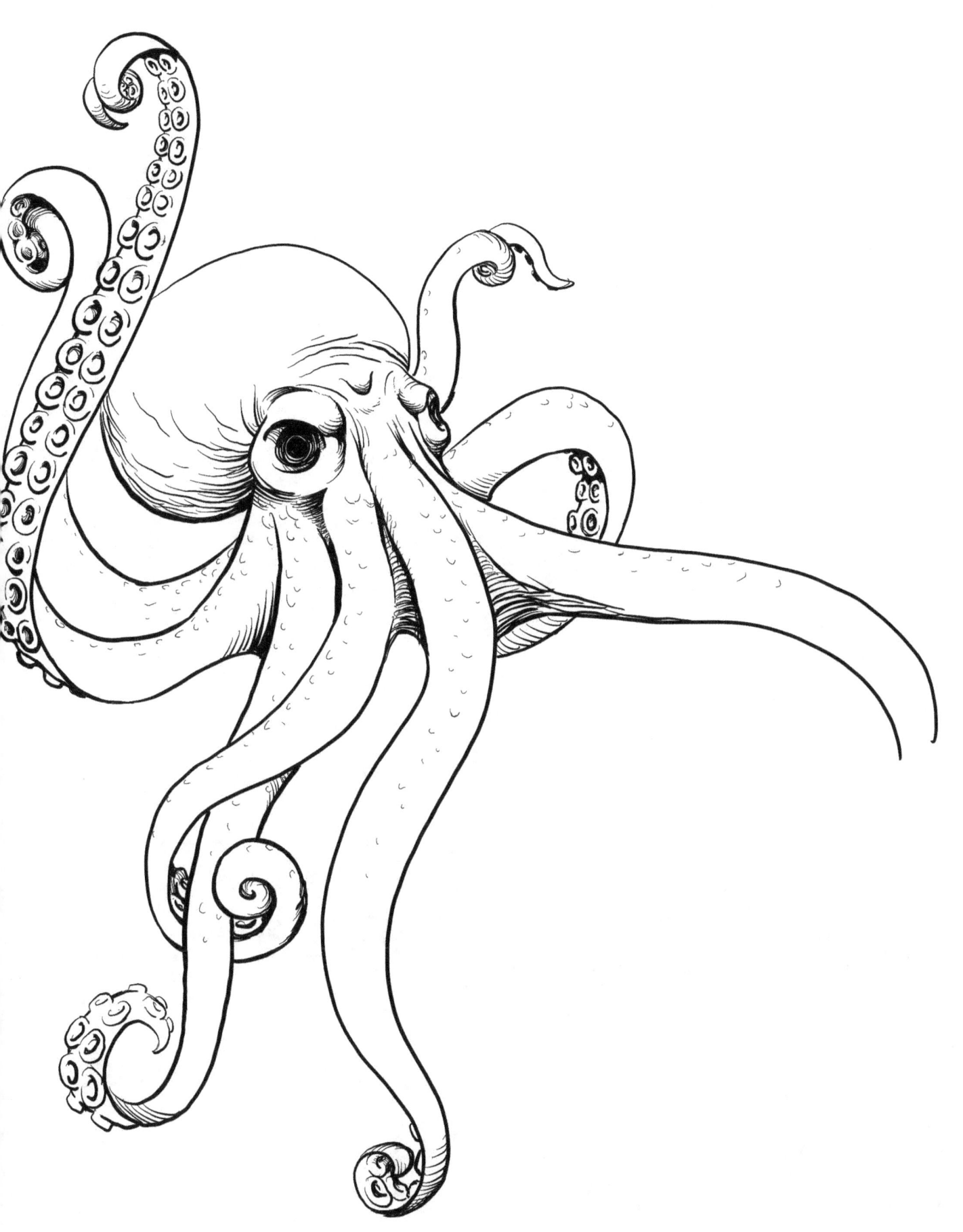

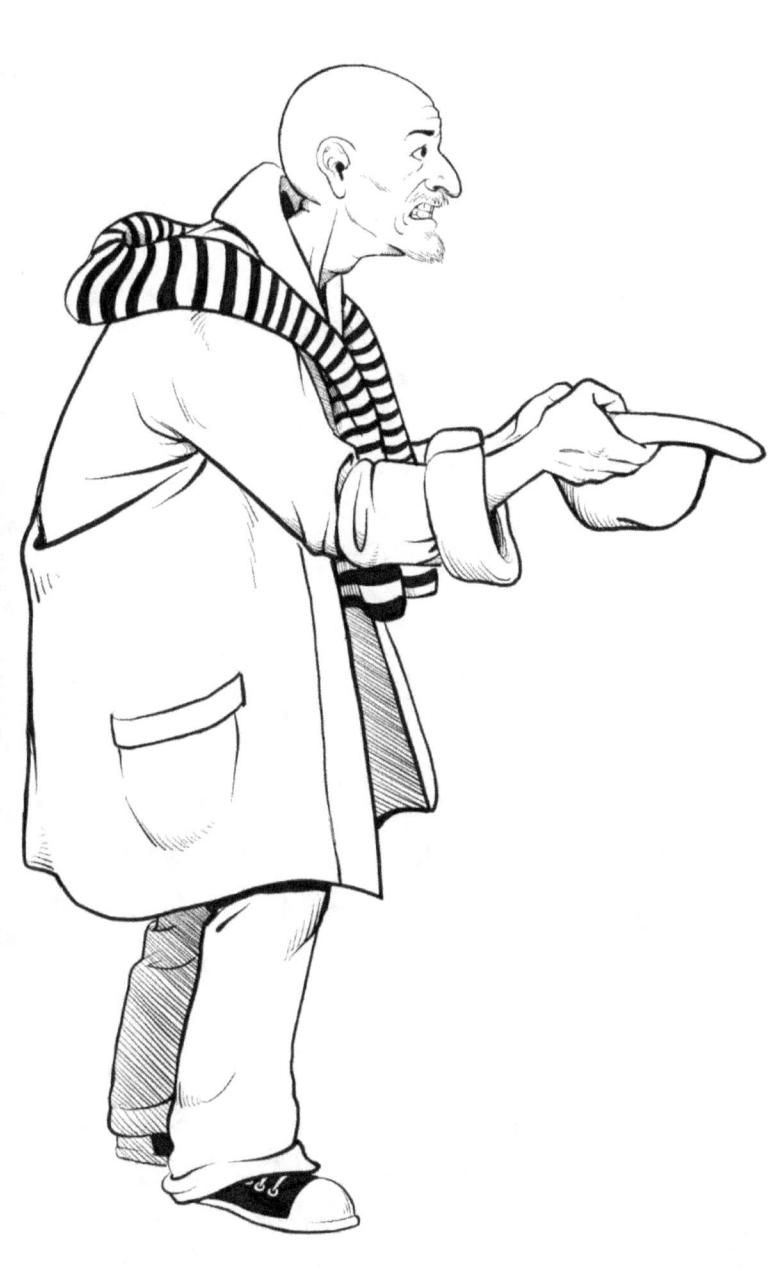

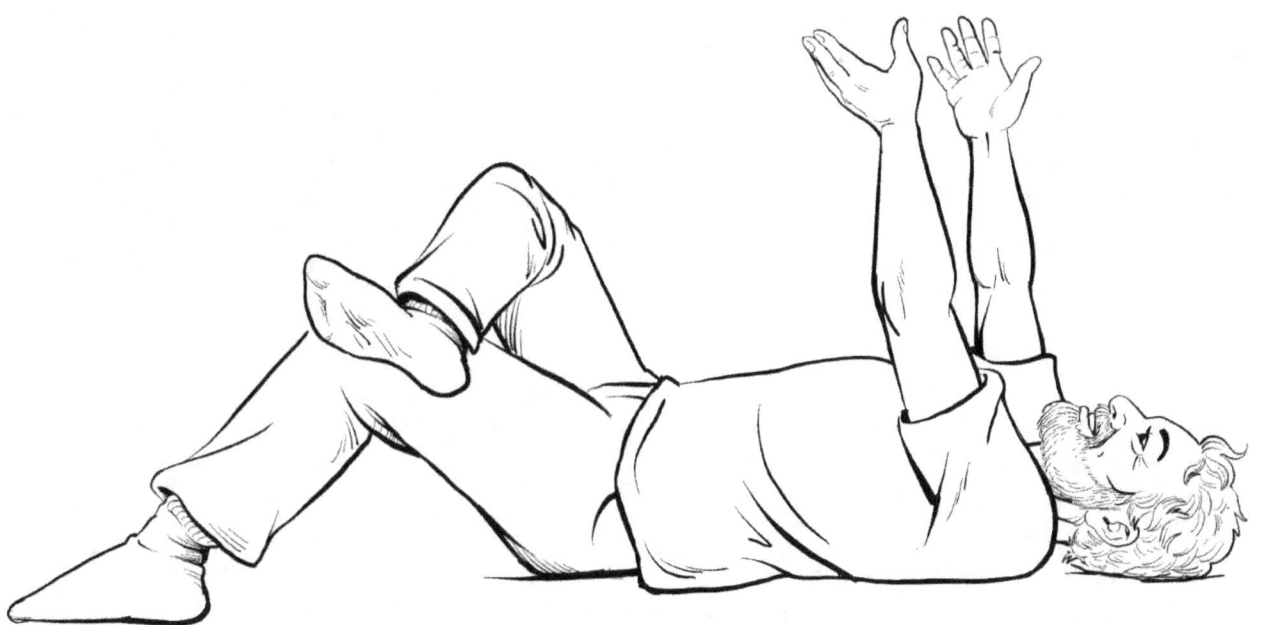

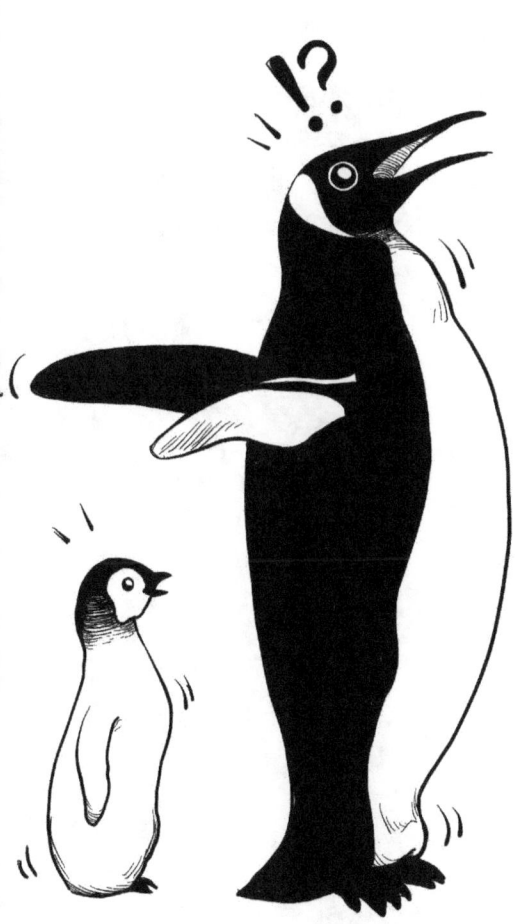

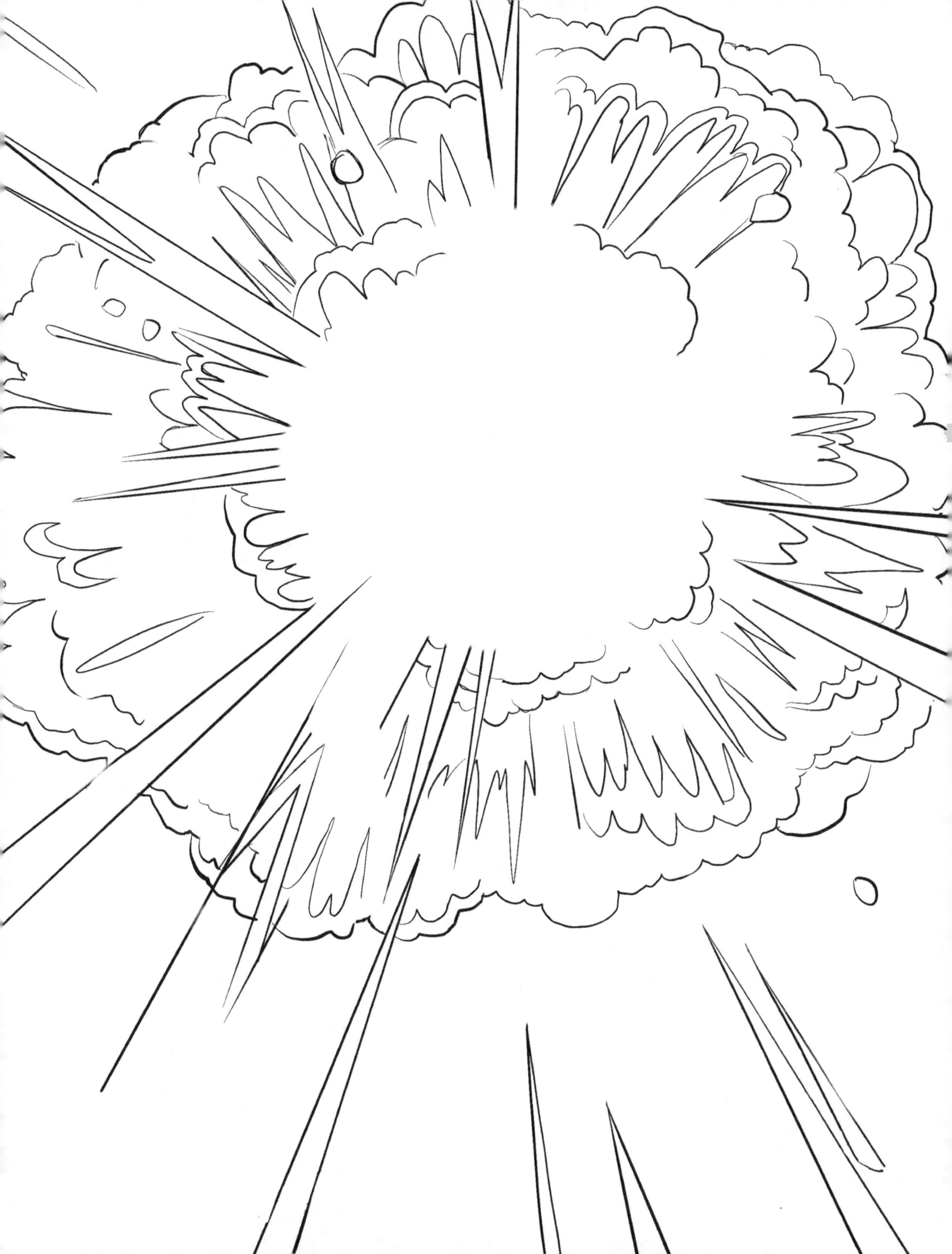

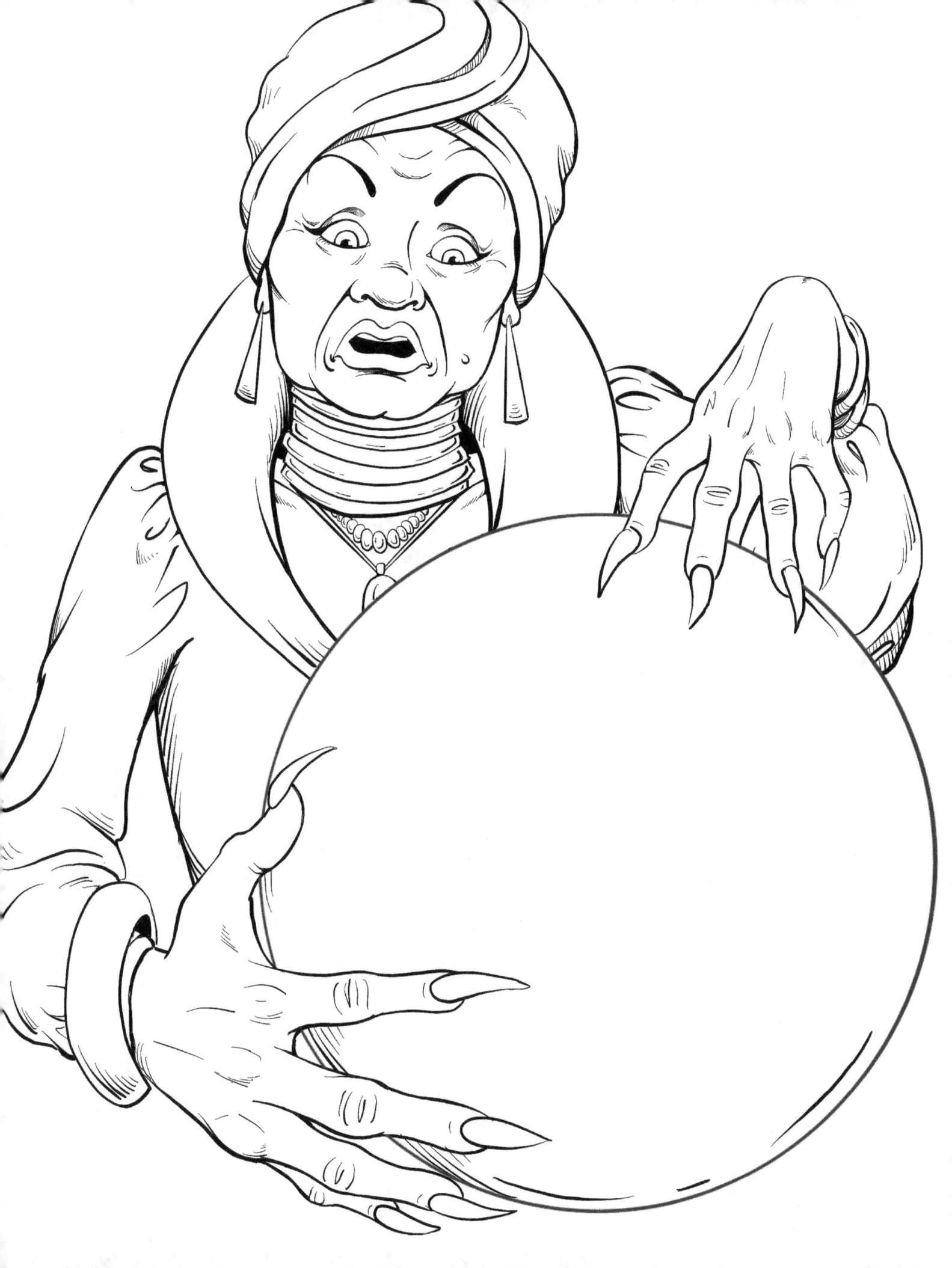

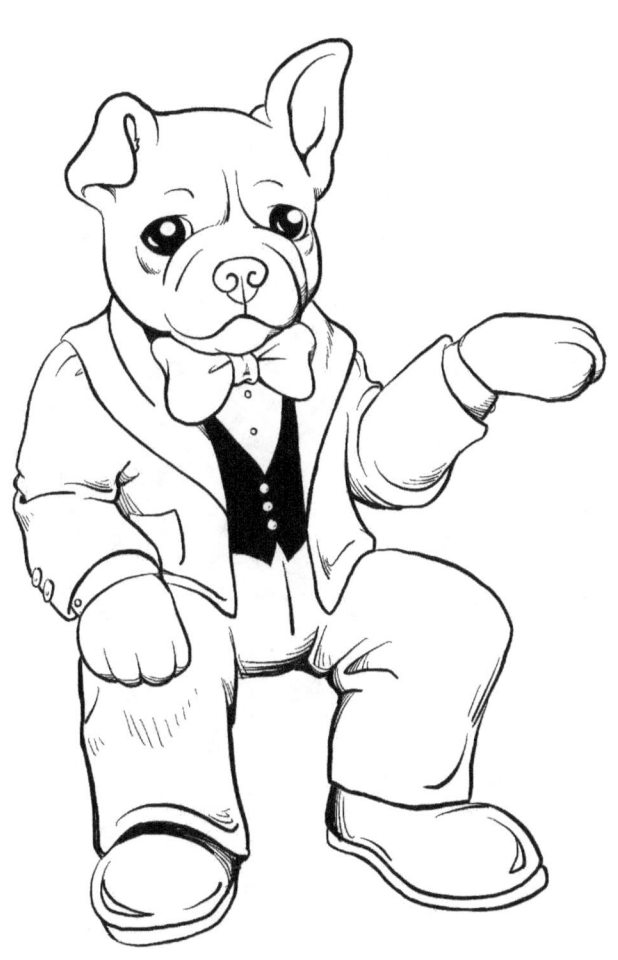

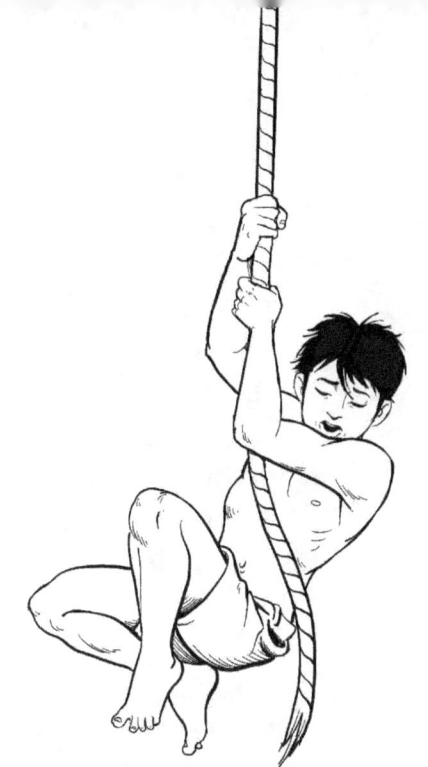

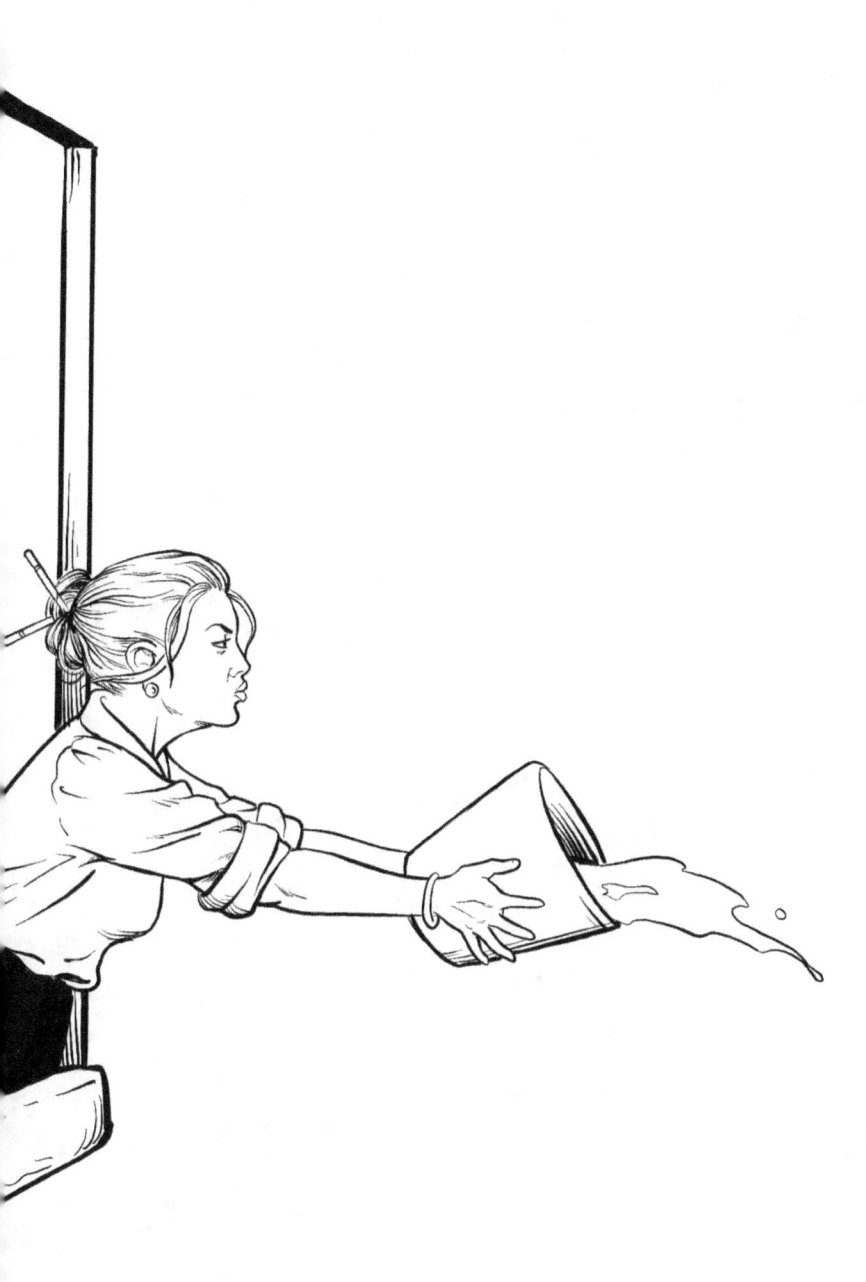

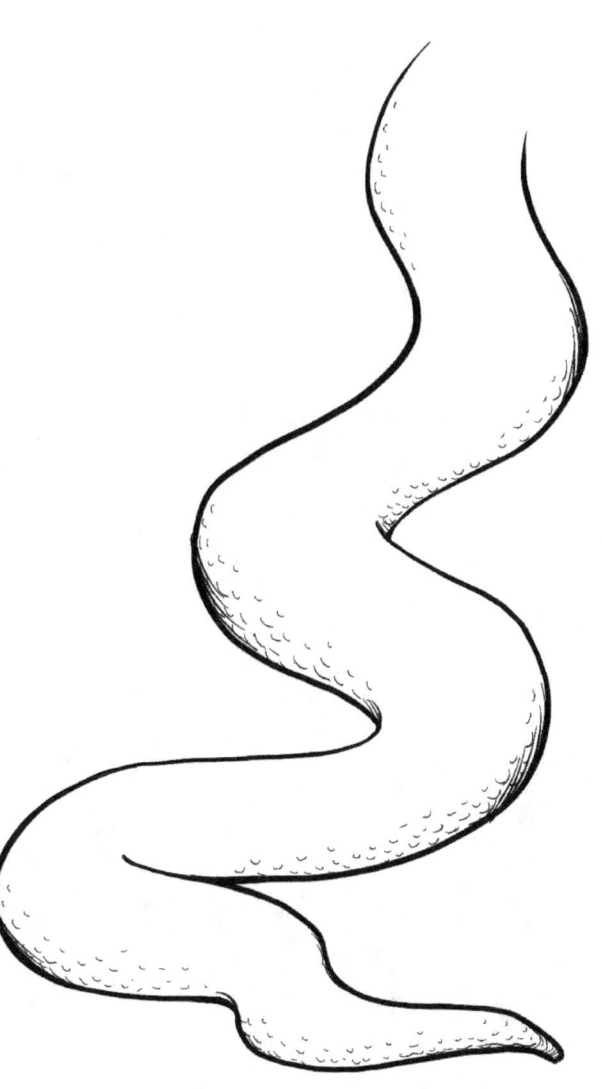

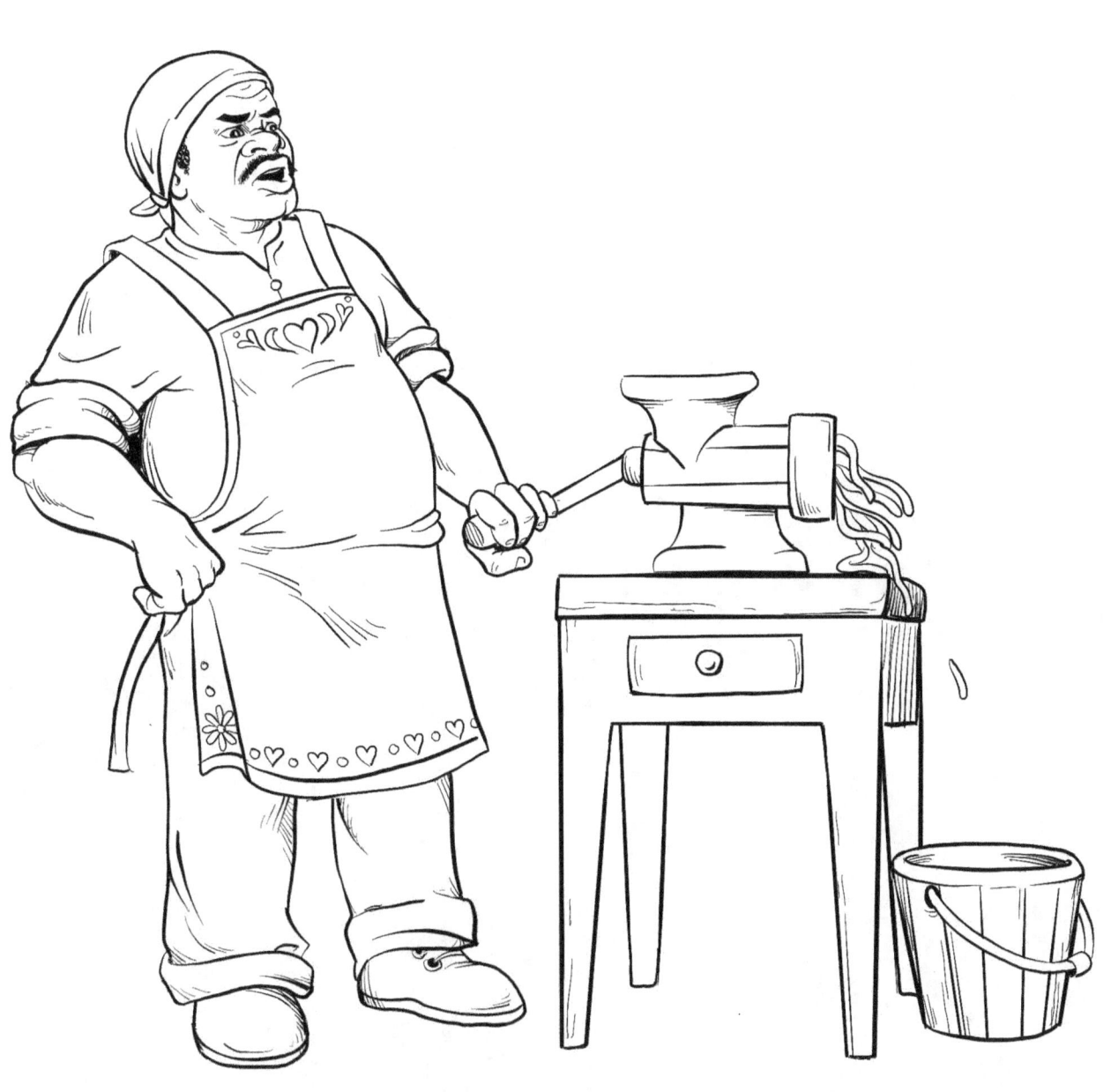

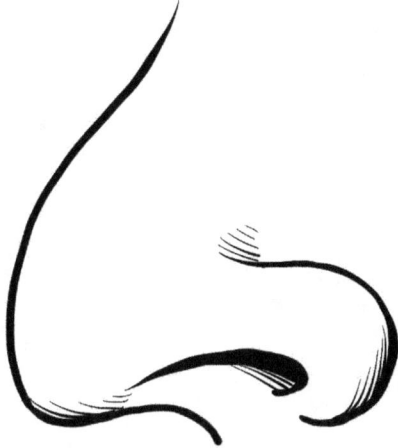

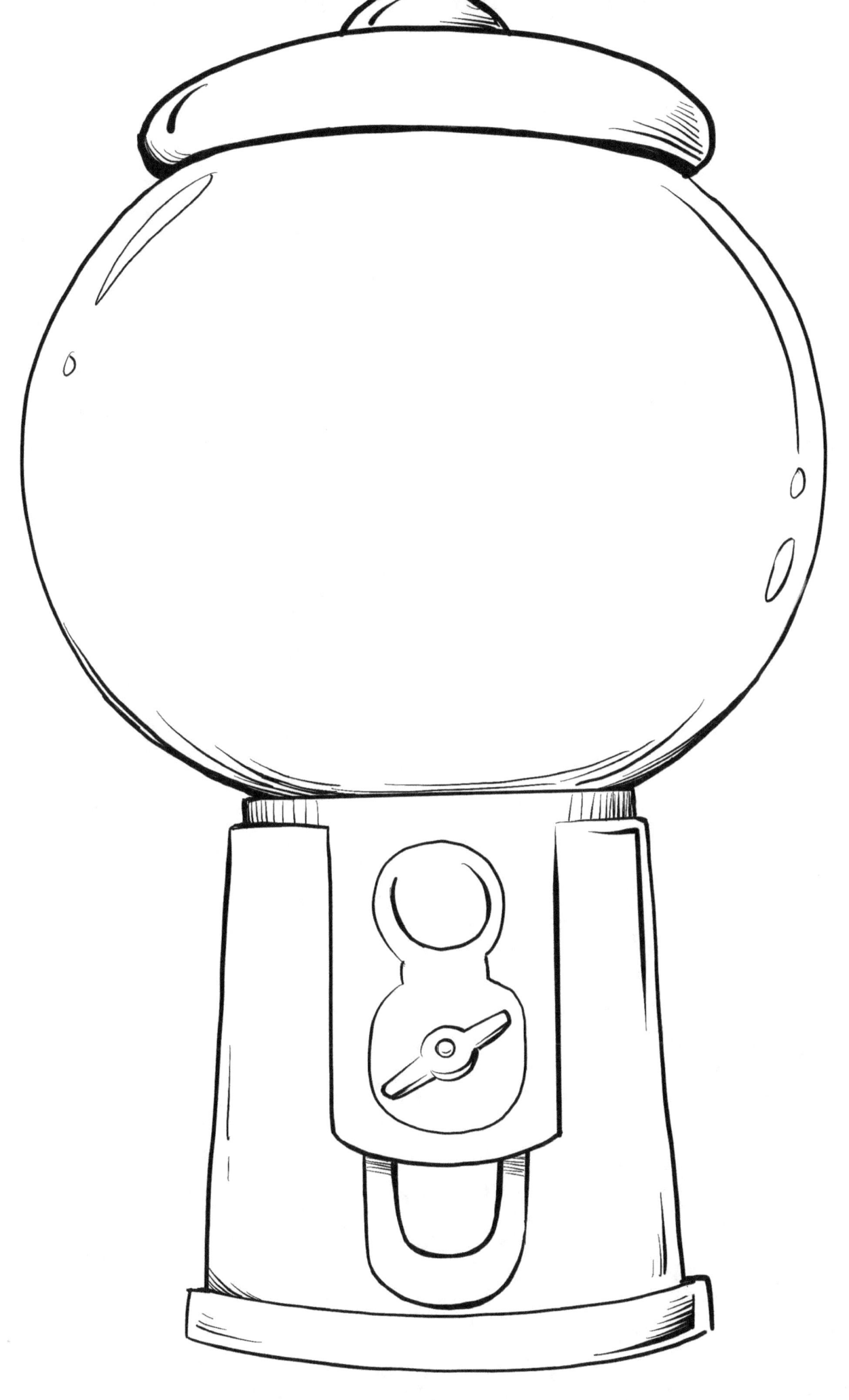

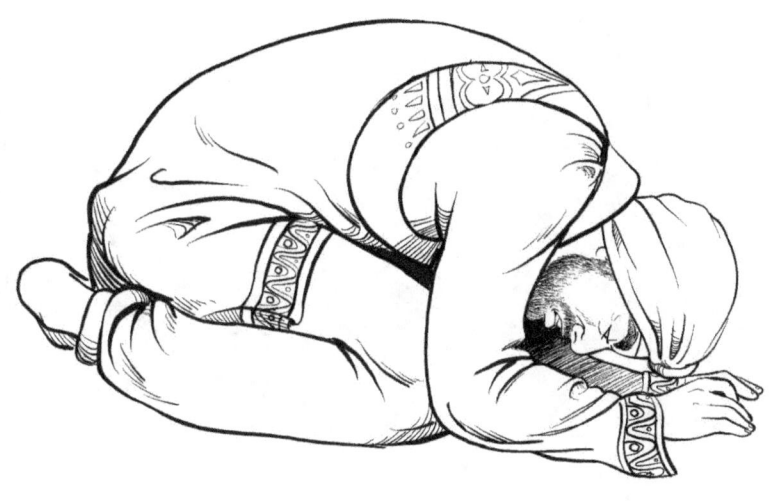

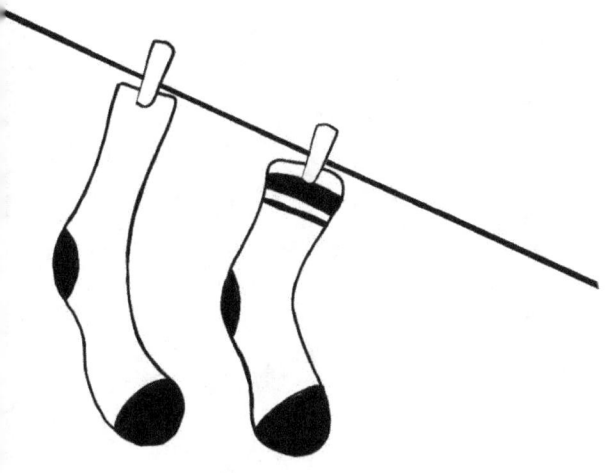
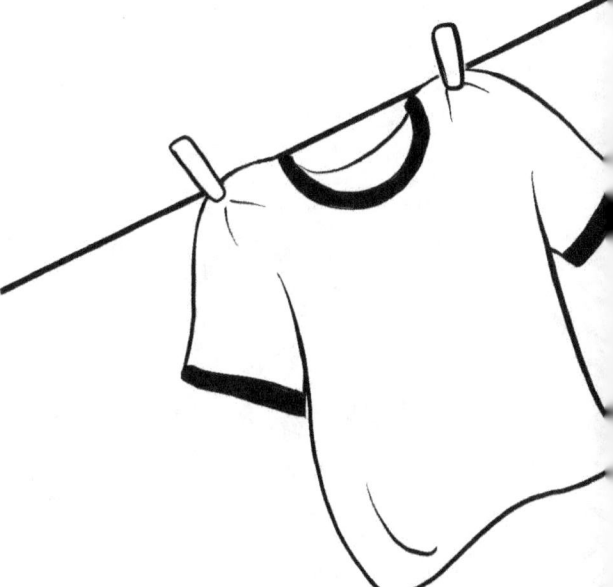

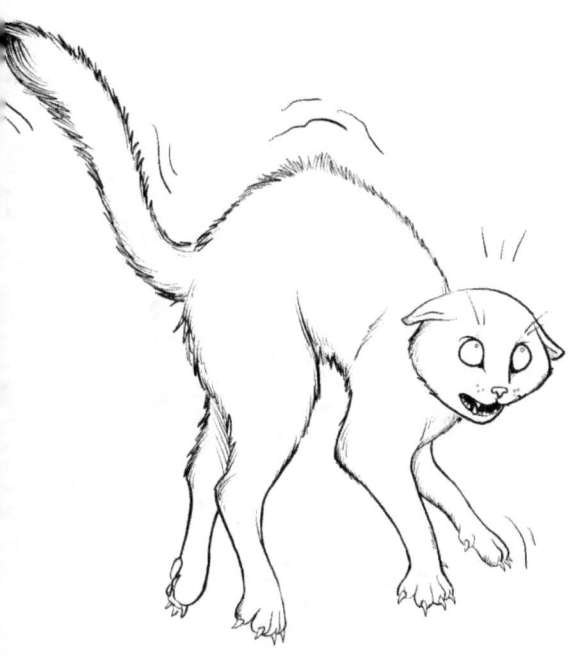

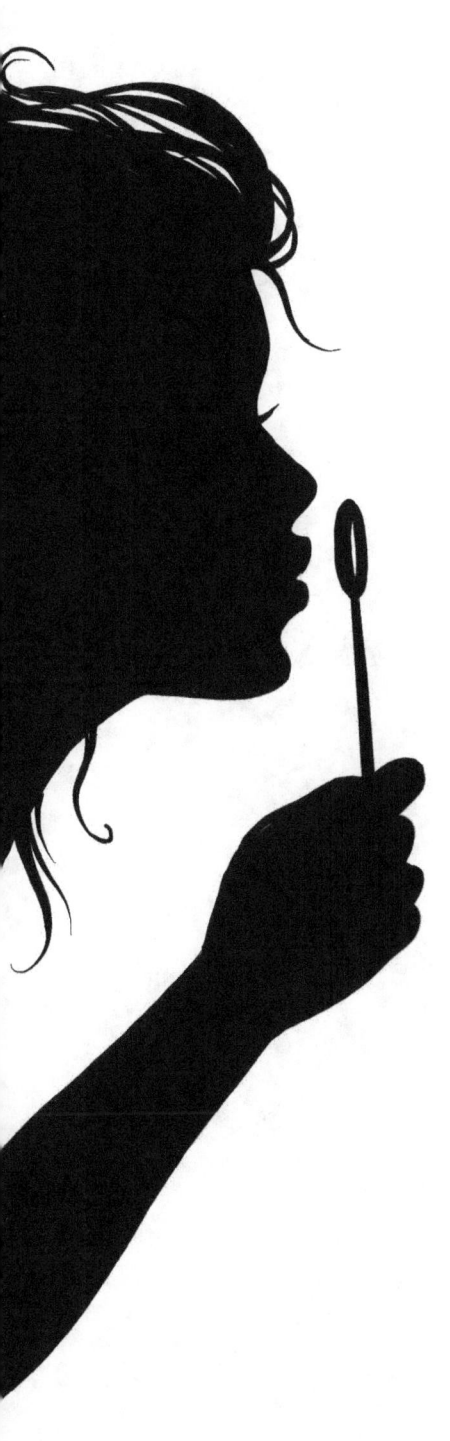

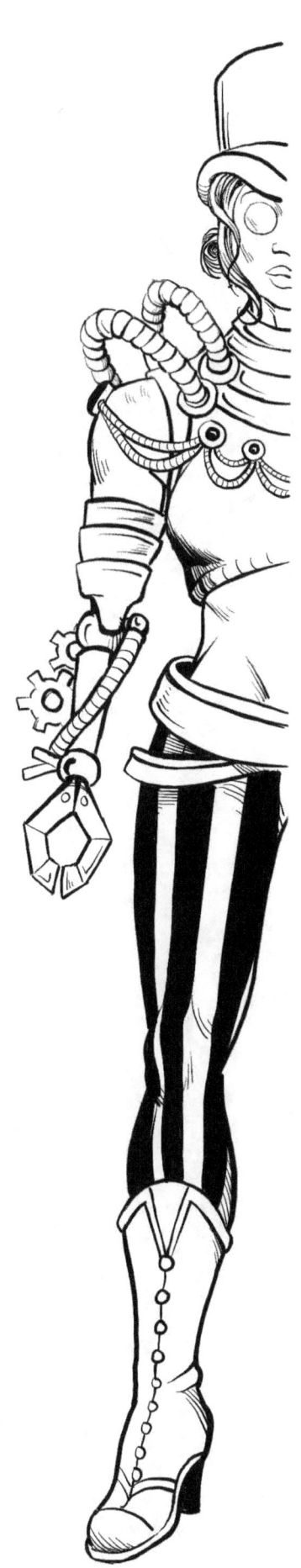

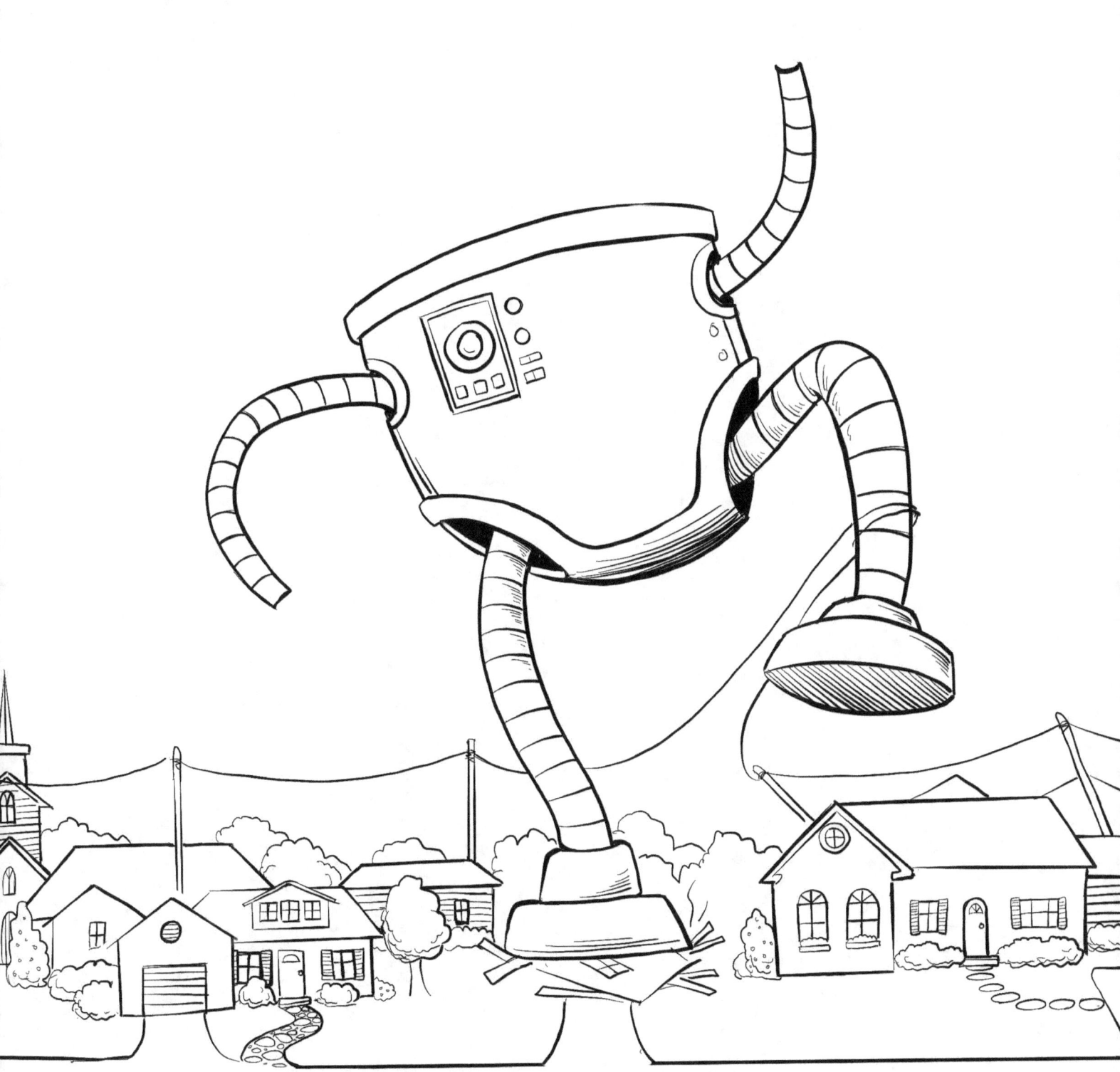

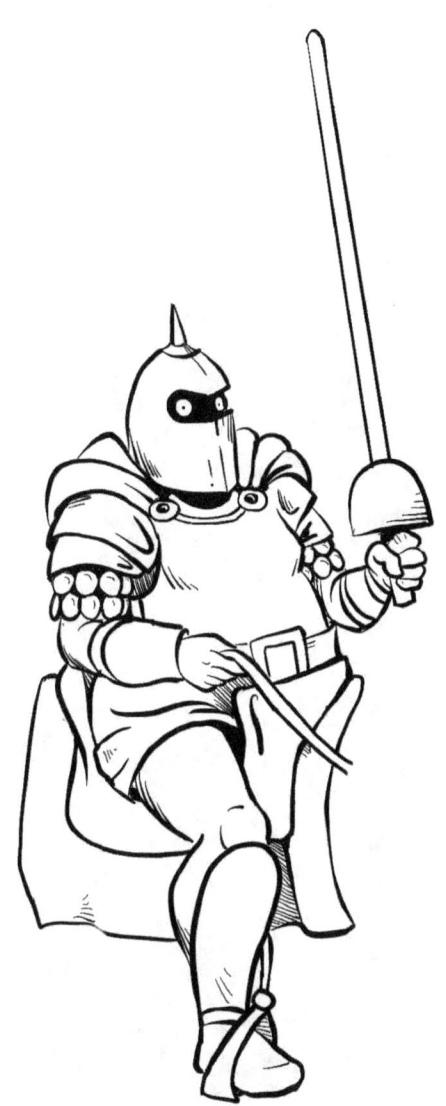

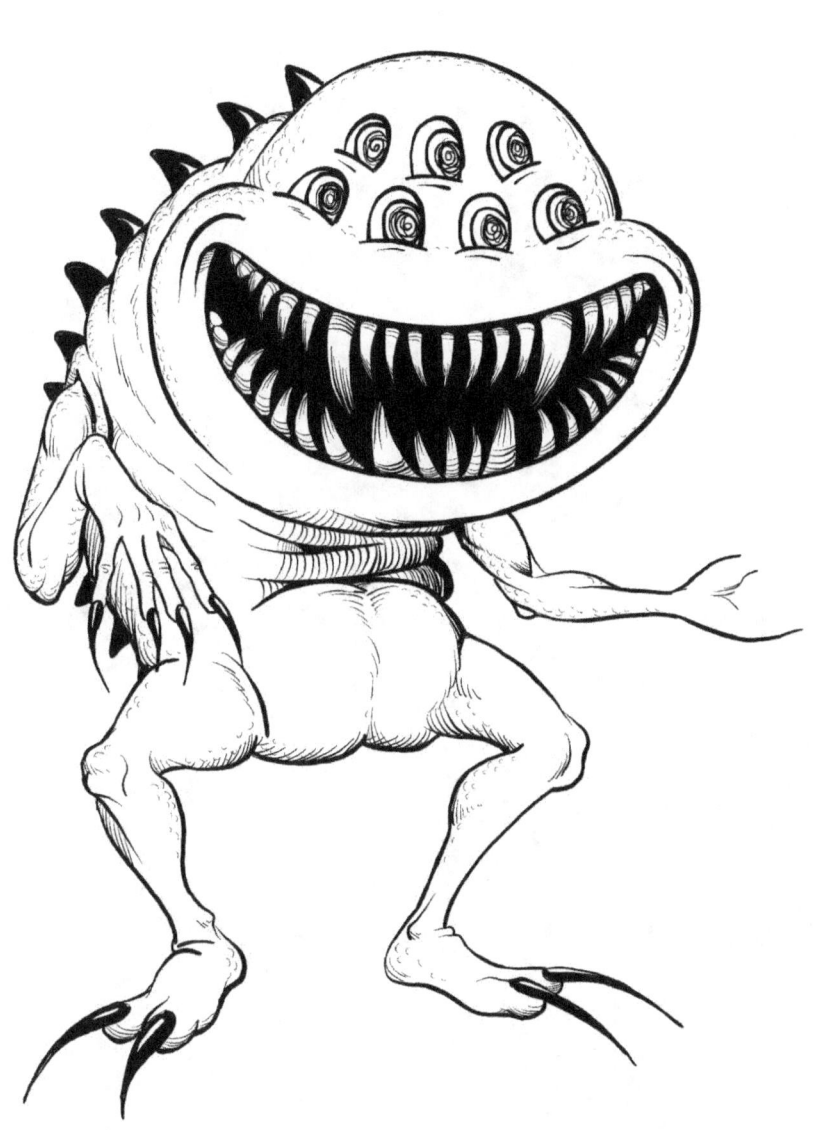

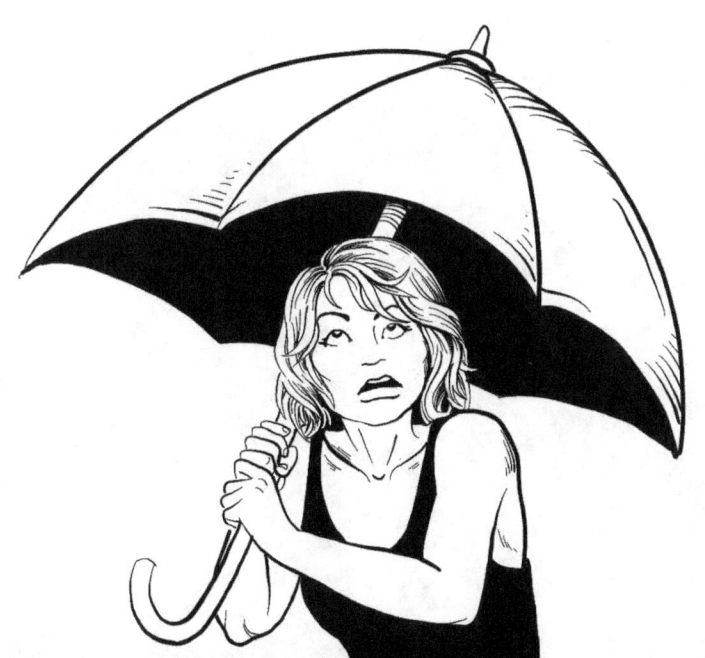

Enjoyed this book?

Be sure to check out volume one...

...and our coloring books too!

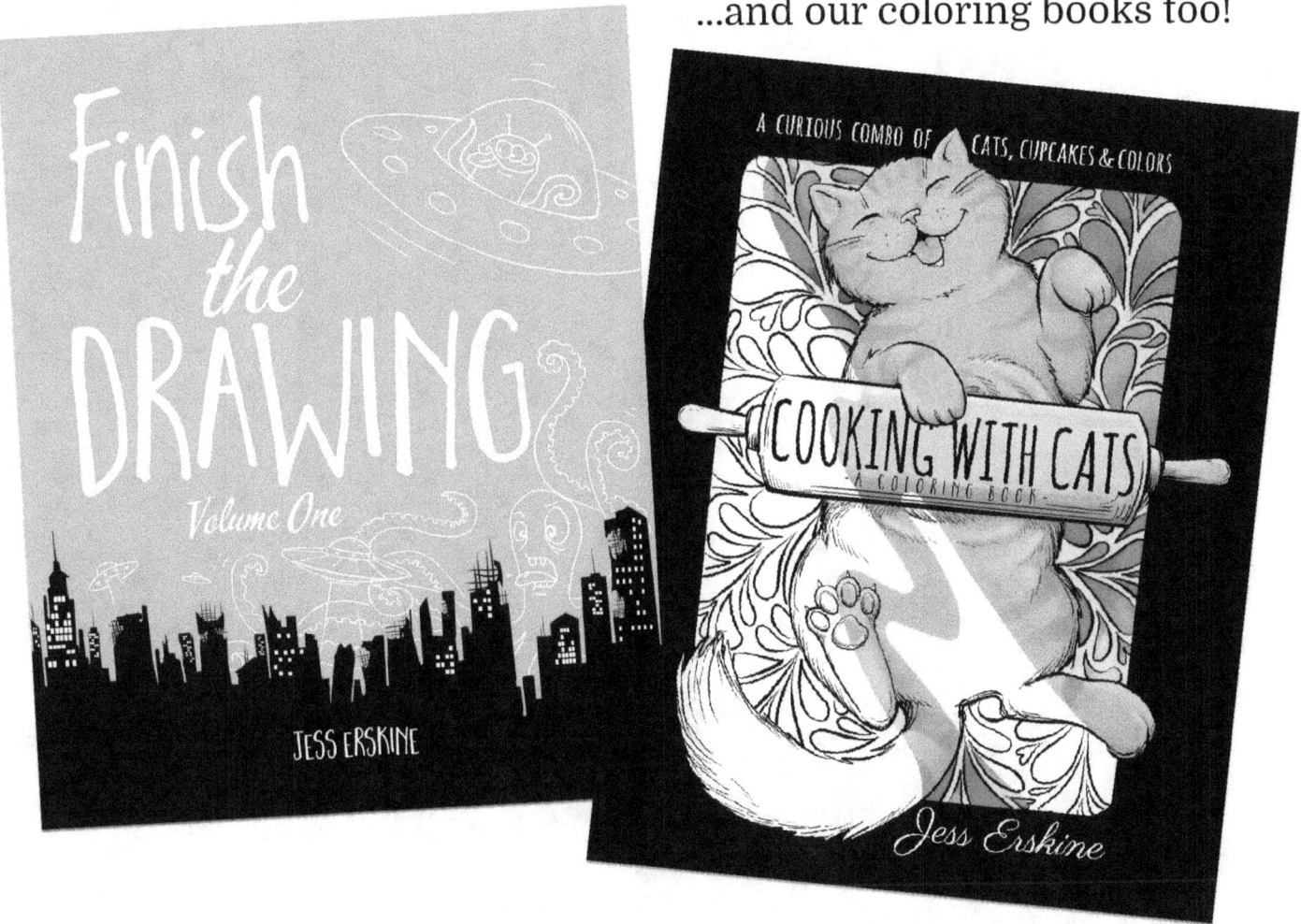

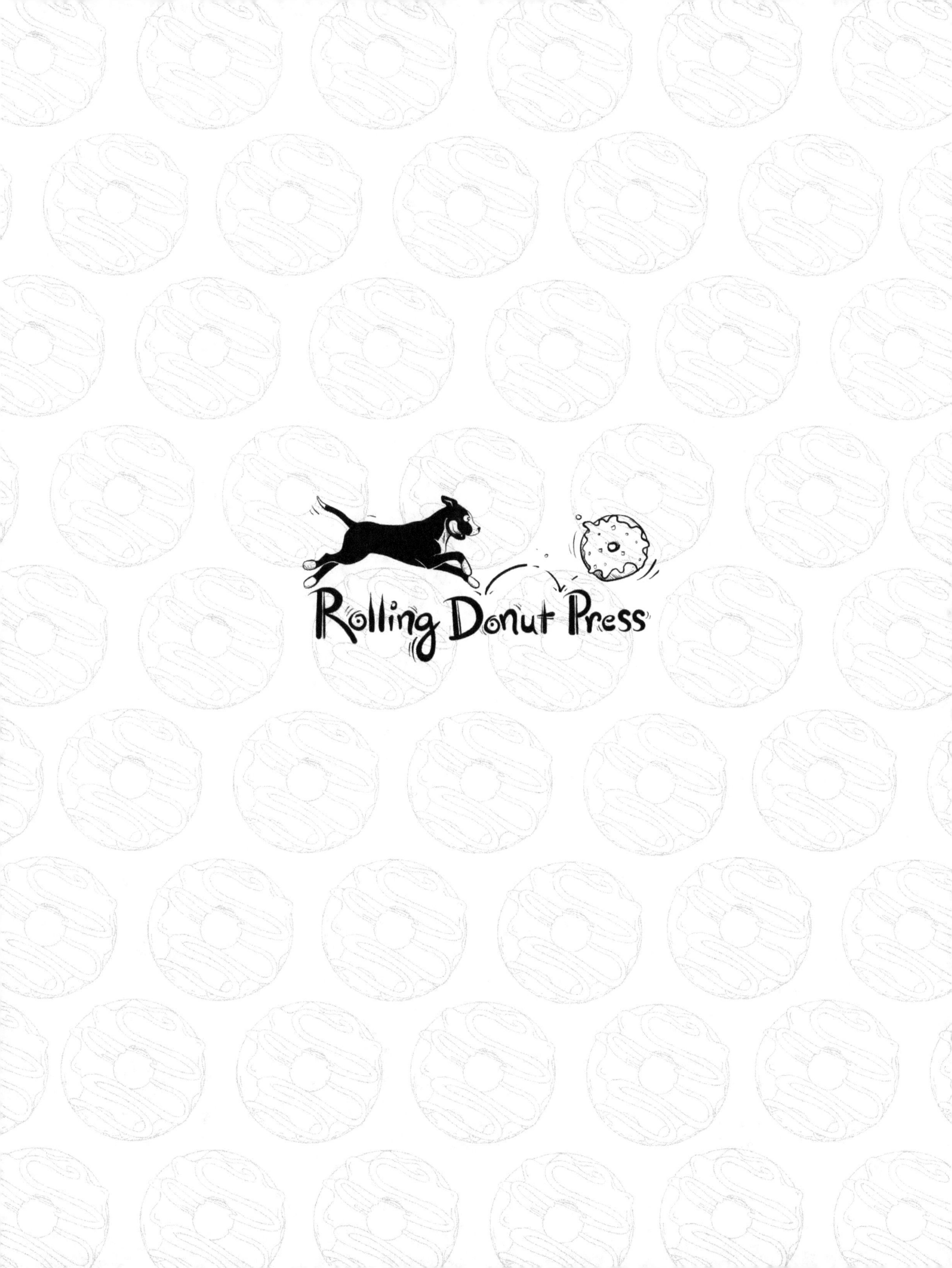